862.3
Vir
Wei

164468

Weiger.
Cristóbal de Virués.

**Learning Resources Center
Nazareth College of Rochester, N. Y.**

TWAYNE'S WORLD AUTHORS SERIES
A Survey of the World's Literature

SPAIN

Gerald E. Wade, Vanderbilt University

EDITOR

Cristóbal de Virués

TWAS 497

Montserrat

CRISTÓBAL DE VIRUÉS

By JOHN G. WEIGER
University of Vermont

TWAYNE PUBLISHERS
A DIVISION OF G. K. HALL & CO., BOSTON

Copyright © 1978 by G. K. Hall & Co.

Published in 1978 by Twayne Publishers,
A Division of G. K. Hall & Co.

All Rights Reserved

Printed on permanent/durable acid-free paper and bound
in the United States of America

First Printing

Library of Congress Cataloging in Publication Data

Weiger, John G.
Cristóbal de Virués.

(Twayne's world authors series ; TWAS 497 : Spain)
Bibliography: p. 155-63
Includes index.
1. Virués, Cristóbal de, fl. 1587—Criticism and interpretation. I.
Series.
PQ6498.V7Z96   862'.3   78-5474
ISBN 0-8057-6338-4

To my Mother and Father

Contents

About the Author
Preface
Acknowledgments
Chronology
1. The Life and Works of Virués — 17
2. The *Monserrate* — 32
3. The Response to Fate and Fortune — 64
4. *Marcela* — 91
5. The Prologues and Epilogues — 115
   Notes and References — 129
   Selected Bibliography — 155
   Index — 164

About the Author

John G. Weiger was born in Dresden, Germany. He received his B.A. from Middlebury College and his M.A. from the University of Colorado. Recipient of a two-year fellowship under the foreign-language provisions of the National Defense Education Act, he studied at Indiana University, where he received his Ph.D. In 1967 Professor Weiger was awarded a Faculty Research Fellowship by the University of Vermont and in 1976-77 he enjoyed a sabbatical leave during which he spent time not only in Spain generally but at the Monastery of Montserrat, site of the epic poem by Virués which the present volume explores.

Dr. Weiger is Professor of Romance Languages at the University of Vermont, where he has taught since 1958. Previously he had served on the faculties of the University of Colorado and Lawrence College (now Lawrence University). From 1964-68, Professor Weiger served as vice-chairman for Spanish of the Department of Romance Languages at the University of Vermont. In the years 1968-71 he served as assistant dean, associate dean, and acting dean of that university's College of Arts and Sciences, subsequently serving the period 1971-76 as Dean of the College of Arts and Sciences. He has also chaired the Modern Language Association's division on the Spanish *comedia* and served on the executive committee of that division.

In addition to numerous articles in journals such as *Hispanófila, Hispania, Philological Quarterly, Romance Notes, Bulletin of the Comediantes,* and others, Professor Weiger's works include papers delivered at the Modern Language Association (1968 and 1976), the University of Kentucky Foreign Language Conference (1968), the National Council of Teachers of English (1974), the Asociación Internacional de Hispanistas (1977) and a series of lectures on Spanish literature of the Golden Age which he was invited to present to the faculty and graduate students of the University of Bologna (1978).

Professor Weiger is author of a previous Twayne volume, *The Valencian Dramatists of Spain's Golden Age* (1976), as well as of

About the Author

Hacia la Comedia: De los valencianos a Lope (Madrid: Planeta, 1978), and *The Individuated Self: Cervantes and the Emergence of the Individual* (Ohio University Press, 1978). He is also the author of "Teaching Foreign Language and Literature," included in *Scholars Who Teach* (Chicago: Nelson-Hall, 1978).

Preface

It is not an uncommon experience for the author of a book to consider the preface one of the more challenging tasks in the composition of the work. Moreover, if it sometimes seems impossible to reduce to prefatory length a concise statement of what the book is about, it is at least equally as difficult to write compendiously of what it is *not* about. Virués is most often studied for his place in the tragedy, the judgment generally corresponding to whether he is perceived as having adhered to Classical precepts, or whether he "failed" in the face of the rising current of the national *comedia*. The present book will not judge him as a success or failure by imposing standards of a genre he evidently did not produce: one tragedy does not a tragedian make, nor does an abundance of deaths provide *a priori* evidence of tragedy. Conversely, the growing popularity of what would later become a national theater cannot be summoned in support of his alleged reluctance to adopt the new styles when evidence of his own participation in that direction supposedly reflected his inability to succeed in the tragedy. If this appears to be circular reasoning — as indeed it is — it nonetheless reflects an accurate perception of Virués's place in the Spanish drama: partly as one of the few to attempt tragedy, partly as one of the precursors of the national *comedia,* but above all as a pivotal figure in an important transitional period of Spain's political and cultural history. It is of no small importance to remember that Virués's works were written between the times of the two great Armadas of the century: Lepanto in 1571, and the "Invincible Armada" of 1588.[1]

If it seemed that the Spanish Empire's political and economic fortune reached its zenith at Lepanto and its nadir in the English Channel, quite the reverse was true of the field of letters. These were the years comprising the first part of Spain's Golden Age of literature. Cervantes and Lope de Vega were only beginning their literary efforts, each in his own way striving to create something appropriate for a new age with an orientation that was at once dependent upon Classical (as well as the more recent Italian) models and eager for its own mode of expression. To speak of an "age" is to have in mind not one or two giants but a host of kindred spirits. In this respect, Virués is to a certain extent more representative of the period than is the author of *Don Quixote* or the "creator" of the *comedia*, for Virués typifies the poets who paved the way and provided the rough outline of the fame which subsequent writers would derive from their efforts with greater works.

It is this transitional and pivotal position which we shall consider as we examine the works of Virués. If he does not occupy a prominent position in the histories of literature, he nonetheless enjoyed the praise and respect of the major figures of his day, as we shall see in detail. Moreover, Virués shares with Guillén de Castro, author of *The Youthful Deeds of the Cid*, the position of being the only members of the Valencian dramatists of Spain's Golden Age who have been subjects of a book-length study. C. V. Sargent's 1930 monograph, *The Dramatic Works of Cristóbal de Virués* (see the Bibliography), concentrated, as its title indicates, primarily on the five dramas, their sources, and the fundamental interpretation of the principal characters. More recently, Alfredo Hermenegildo has devoted lengthy sections of two books to Virués: *Los trágicos españoles del siglo XVI* and *La tragedia en el renacimiento español*. The titles of these two volumes reveal their intent: the works are examined principally in their function as tragedies. On a smaller scale in a previous Twayne volume, *The Valencian Dramatists of Spain's Golden Age,* I attempted to relate Virués's dramas to the development of the honor code as it evolved in the pre-Lopean theater of the sixteenth century. From yet another perspective, portions of my more recent *Hacia la Comedia: De los valencianos a Lope* focus on the understanding of the drama as a genre to be heard (more than seen) and on the use of imagery to link opening and closing scenes. Finally, no introduction to Virués's place in the Spanish drama is complete without mention of the seminal work by Rinaldo Froldi, whose *Il teatro valenzano e l'origine della commedia barocca* (1962; Spanish translation, 1968) placed Virués and his fellow Valencians in a perspective which had previously been denied them by the persistence of a myth with respect to the creation of an entire genre.

The present volume, as a result, will repeat neither the intent nor the content of the works just enumerated. In the dramas, we shall be concerned less with tragedy specifically and more with the transition to a newer attitude toward theater generally. Moreover,

Preface

inasmuch as Virués's literary production is not limited to the drama but includes the lengthy heroic poem, *El Monserrate,* we shall devote an extensive analysis to this often praised and rarely discussed work. Although no knowledge of Spanish on the part of the reader is required or assumed, a limited number of passages have been reproduced in the original (usually followed by an English rendition) for purposes other than a comprehension of the content, for example, in order to illustrate Virués's use of rhyme or an onomatopoetic device. The translations into English are my own unless otherwise indicated.

JOHN G. WEIGER

*Budalona, Spain, and
Shelburne, Vermont*

Acknowledgments

Expressions of gratitude in the prefatory pages of a book may be considered standard procedure. However, the following names belong to people whose patience, help, and encouragement have been anything but routine. To Janet W. Díaz, I owe appreciation for her initial confidence in my endeavor; to Gerald E. Wade, much gratitude for the helpful and discerning suggestions and the benefit of his critical advice. A special note of thanks is due John L. Buechler, head of special collections at the Bailey Library of the University of Vermont, for his kind assistance in making available some indispensable material from the eighteenth and nineteenth centuries as well as for maintaining in his area of the library an environment truly conducive to the pursuit of scholarly endeavors. A very similar measure of gratitude must be expressed to Theodore S. Beardsley, Jr., director of the Hispanic Society of America, for the invaluable aid in examining the Society's collection of Virués's works, particularly in the matter of dating the *Monserrate.*

That I should have the opportunity to write this work almost literally in the shadow of Montserrat is the result of kindness and hospitality shown me by my uncle, Enrique Weiger of Barcelona, who allowed me to live and write for nearly half a year in nearby Badalona, with the Mediterranean at my feet and Montserrat above my head. As the chapter on that topic details, to write between sea and mountain (particularly that sea and that mountain) is not without its significance. Furthermore, to be able to visit the awesome and magnificent setting of the monastery among the towering rocks was in itself an experience for which I shall always be grateful. Gratitude and appreciation are also due Señorita Remedios Montes Meléndez of Barcelona. "Remi" provided friendship and humor while clarifying ambiguities of language and serving as my guide through the monastery at Montserrat. Finally, a very special acknowledgment to my wife, Leslie, who not only typed and retyped the manuscript while holding a full-time job as someone else's secretary, but whose own interest in literature helped make this book a shared venture.

Chronology

1547 Birth of Cervantes.
1550? Birth of Virués.
1556 Accession of Philip II.
1558 Death of Charles V.
1562 Birth of Lope de Vega.
1563 Final session of the Council of Trent.
1571 Battle of Lepanto.
1573 Battle of Tunis.
1578 Death of Don John of Austria.
1585 Publication of Cervantes's *Galatea* (contains first major published reference to Virués).
1587 Publication of the first edition of the *Monserrate*.
1588 Defeat of the Spanish Armada. First visit of Lope de Vega to Valencia.
1598 Death of Philip II. Second visit of Lope de Vega to Valencia.
1600 Birth of Calderón.
1602 Publication of *El Monserrate segundo* in Milan.
1604 Publication of Lope de Vega's *Rimas*, headed by a laudatory poem by Virués.
1605 Publication of Part I of *Don Quixote*. Second reference by Cervantes to Virués's work.
1609 Publication of Virués's *Obras trágicas y líricas*. Publication of the third edition of the *Monserrate*. Publication of the second edition of Lope de Vega's *Rimas*, together with the *Arte nuevo de hacer comedias en este tiempo*.
1614 Publication of Cervantes's *Viaje del Parnaso* (contains third published tribute by Cervantes to Virués).
1615 Publication of Part II of *Don Quixote*.
1616 Death of Cervantes and of Shakespeare.
1630 Publication of Lope de Vega's *Laurel de Apolo* (contains significant praise of Virués's works).

CHAPTER 1

The Life and Works of Virués

I *A Day in the Life of a Spanish Author*

ON Sunday, October 7, 1571, one of the most meaningful battles in the history of mankind was fought. Under the command of Don John of Austria, illegitimate son of the Emperor Charles V, the fleet of the Holy League (Spain, Venice, and the Papacy) sailed into Greek waters and destroyed the Ottoman naval force. It was the battle of Lepanto.

If we have not said that it was crucial or that it altered the course of history in and of itself, we have nonetheless described it as meaningful. For it was, and would continue to be, replete with meaning. Historians will debate its immediate and ultimate military and political consequences, but even the best of them confesses his confusion about these matters. What took place on that particular day seems clear; what occurred thereafter is also a matter of record. The cause and effect relationship, however, remains debatable: "Lepanto was the most spectacular military event in the Mediterranean during the entire sixteenth century. Dazzling triumph of courage and naval technique though it was, it is hard to place convincingly in a conventional historical perspective."[1] In a similar vein, Elliott concludes that the "spectacular victory of the Christian forces at Lepanto in 1571 was to epitomize for contemporaries all that was most glorious in the crusade against Islam. It was an eternal source of pride to those who, like Miguel de Cervantes, had fought in the battle and could show the scar of their wounds.... The trophies of battle were proudly displayed, and the victory was commemorated in pictures, medals, and tapestries. But, in fact, the battle of Lepanto proved a curiously deceptive triumph...."[2]

Debatable as the political consequences may be,[3] the effect upon the imagination is beyond dispute, as even the sampling above reveals in the historians' use of words like "spectacular," "dazzling," and "glorious." Small wonder that Cervantes would bestow upon himself the epithet of *el manco de Lepanto* (the cripple of Lepanto). The future author of *Don Quixote* was twenty-four, perhaps two or three years older than another budding Spanish writer who was also wounded that day in the same battle. As was Cervantes, Cristóbal de Virués was the son of a physician. As would Cervantes, Virués would always retain the impression made upon him by the tumultuous events of that October Sunday in 1571. On more than one occasion Virués would refer specifically to his memories of Lepanto, and in a more indirect fashion the significance of the event would influence the form as well as the content of his poetry. And it was his poetry that would immortalize him: ironically, not because of his works in their own right but because his compatriot in the armada of Lepanto was to rescue him from oblivion by mentioning his name in *Don Quixote:* the curate would spare Virués's epic *El Monserrate* in the famous scrutiny of Don Quixote's library: "And here we have three more [said the barber]...: the *Araucana* of Don Alonso de Ercilla; the *Austriada* of Juan Rufo, magistrate of Cordova; and the *Monserrate* of Cristóbal de Virués, the poet of Valencia."

"These three books," said the curate, "are the best that have been written in the Castilian tongue and may well compete with the most famous of Italy; keep them as the richest jewels of poetry that Spain has to show."[4]

As we shall see, the other literary giant of the time, Lope de Vega, who participated in that later armada of 1588, would also mention Virués and similarly preserve our poet's name thereby. Ironically, it was Virués who "expected his [own] verse to bring immortality to the friends it praised."[5]

II *Biographical Résumé*

We still remain uncertain of Virués's birthdate, not an uncommon gap in the biography of many a better-known figure. Perhaps more surprisingly, the date of his death remains conjectural as well. We might attribute this to his being of lesser renown than some of his contemporaries, such as Cervantes (1547–1616), Lope de Vega (1562-1635), or his fellow Valencian, Guillén de Castro (1569–1631), yet we do possess more accurate vital statistics about others whose works are of lesser consequence. In point of fact,

The Life and Works of Virués

Virués's literary efforts were considered indeed to be of considerable consequence by his contemporaries (including the three notables just mentioned), which is one of the reasons that we should find it profitable to take a prolonged look at his work.

It is generally agreed that Cristóbal de Virués was born in Valencia in 1550.[6] On the other hand, there is a disagreement of some interest with respect to the year of the poet's death. The pieces of the puzzle are related to the three names mentioned above. Although some believe that Virués died in 1609 or 1610,[7] a number of scholars have given careful scrutiny to some laudatory verses by Cervantes and Lope de Vega, as a result of which they have deduced that Virués was still living in 1614. In that year Cervantes — himself only two years from death — published his *Viaje del Parnaso,* a poem which praises a large number of contemporary authors, including a quartet of Valencian poets: Castro, Aguilar,[8] Ferrer, and Virués. In view of the fact that these poets are grouped together by Cervantes, Cejador has concluded that they were all living in 1613 or 1614 when Cervantes composed (presumably) and published his poem.[9] This must scarcely be taken as conclusive by itself, nor must the similar comment by Martí Grajales to the effect that the mention of Virués among his contemporaries, with no allusion to his having died, mean that he was still alive at that time.

The case appears strengthened by Sargent's observation of Cervantes's use of the present tense in the verb *criar:* "Certainly the use of *cría* in present tense implies that they are living...."[10] However, as my translation in note 8 indicates, this verb is not limited to a particular present; rather, it expresses a general observation about a "famous group *of the sort* [the river] Turia raises." The verb, therefore, may be used neither to support nor to refute any assumptions about Virués being alive or dead in 1614, particularly when we compare the passage from the *Viaje del Parnaso* with a similar one from Cervantes's pastoral novel, *La Galatea* (1585), in which the tense, as well as the sense, leaves no doubt about our poet's vitality: "Cristóbal de Virués, your knowledge and valor so exceed your years...."[11] At the other extreme, there can be no question that Virués had died before 1630, when Lope de Vega wrote:

> In the lovely city which the Turia bathes,
> this funereal and glorious remembrance
> might not suffice to honor Captain Virués.
> Oh unique genius! Rest in peace, you,

to whom the Comic Muses owed
the best beginnings they did behold.
Celebrated tragedies wrote you.[12]

Despite the obvious references to Virués's having died, the first line cited is almost identical to that of Cervantes's 1614 poem: Lope also refers to Valencia as the city which the Turia bathes (present tense).[13] In short, we have no evidence that Virués died in 1609 or 1610, as some would have it; nor do we have documentation that he was still alive in 1614, although we can confirm an undisputed fact: by 1630 Virués was no longer among the living. Most significantly, the above reveals a good deal about the esteem in which the poet was held by the major artists of his time, a subject to which we shall return below.

Of no small importance for our understanding of Cristóbal's cultural background is the distinguished family in which he grew up. His father, Alonso de Virués, was not only a distinguished doctor of medicine (he was personal physician to Juan de Ribera, archbishop of Valencia), but a man of letters and friend of Juan Luis Vives, the famous humanist. A document of historical interest is a letter written (in Latin) by Vives to Erasmus which mentions Alonso several times.[14] Cristóbal's sister, Jerónima Agustina Benita, is reputed to have been an expert in Latin,[15] and a brother, Francisco, was a doctor of theology and a poet as well. The latter's early death prompted Cristóbal to write a eulogistic sonnet. Another brother followed in their father's footsteps: a physician and poet, Dr. Jerónimo de Virués was a member of the famous literary society the *Academia de los Nocturnos* (Academy of the Nocturnals), whose *Cancionero* contains a number of his works.[16] Although Jerónimo is not the subject of our study, the topics of some of the works he composed for the academy are of interest inasmuch as they relate to themes developed by his brother, as we shall note in subsequent chapters. Among Jerónimo's compositions we find one which debates whether it is better to be fortunate or wise; another that considers which is strongest: king, wine, woman, or truth; still another debates which is the most advantageous to the republic: the study of letters or the study of arms.[17] Ebersole believes it safe to assume that Jerónimo's membership in the *Academia de los Nocturnos* attracted Cristóbal to several meetings of the academy, but he cites no evidence in support of his supposition.[18] Eduardo Juliá Martínez finds the explanation of the charac-

The Life and Works of Virués

teristics of Cristóbal's works specifically in his having spent the greater part of his life away from Valencia. In this connection, Juliá points out that Cristóbal de Virués was the only Valencian dramatist of the time who did not participate in the *Academia de los Nocturnos*.[19]

One of his absences is accounted for by his participation in the battle of Lepanto. That he participated personally is underscored on various occasions. In the *Monserrate* (ironically published in 1587, on the eve of the "invincible" armada),[20] he not only tells us that he was at Lepanto, but expresses his humility as a poet before "the greatest victory known to the world." If only he could describe it as he saw it: "Oh, if Heaven to my pen were to concede / what here my person it allowed to see!"[21] His pen did not fail him, however, in an eclogue which he wrote on the same subject. I reproduce here the original Spanish as well as an English rendition not only because the isolated poem has a bearing on his other writings, as may be seen by a comparison with an excerpt from one of the dramas, but because the acoustic effect of the original is significant in itself. First a segment from the eclogue:

> *Rumores, alaridos, voces fieras,*
> *clamores por el aire resonaron,*
> *el cual, herido de las balas, brama*
> *entre el humo, las flechas y la llama.*
> *La luz oscureció la nube espesa,*
> *el ancho mar se revolvió alterado,*
> *aturde el son que con terrible priesa*
> *se forma en el metal duro y templado;*
> *quien a cual con la flecha le atraviesa,*
> *y quien es de una bala traspasado,*
> *quien en el hondo mar se arroja ardiendo,*
> *y quien trabaja por matar muriendo.*[22]

> (Rumblings, howlings, fiendish voices,
> clamorous noises through the air resounded,
> which, by bullets wounded, bellows
> amid smoke, arrows and the flame
> The light obscured by heavy cloud,
> the upset broad sea billowed,
> the din which stuns with quickened pace
> on tough and tempered metal sounds;
> cleft is one whom the arrow crushes,
> quartered is he whom the bullet clouts,

killed he who flaming seeks the brine,
a corpse who strives to kill while dying.)

I have attempted, in my rendition, to capture the following aspects of the original: the initial impression of war which Virués conveys is one of noise; the substance of war is its rapid, repeated, varied yet ubiquitous pain and death;[23] there is an onomatopoetic quality, particularly in the last four lines cited, which, combined with the alliterative velar sound, reproduces the clangor of war.[24] I have endeavored to convey this last effect by my use of "cleft," "crushes," "quartered," "clouts," "killed," and "corpse" in the corresponding lines.

This dual impact of the cacophony and torment of war upon the sensibilities of the young poet-scholar would remain with him throughout his life. In *La gran Semíramis* (Great Semíramis) he resorts to the same devices:

> ¡Qué compasión el grito de los niños;
> qué terneza los llantos de los viejos;
> qué horror la muerte de los fuertes mozos;
> qué temor la braveza y furia airada
> de las crueles armas vencedoras,
> de las gentes indómitas feroces;
> qué confusión el diligente saco;
> el bullicioso ardiente y fiero robo
> de la cruel y codiciosa gente;
> qué espanto, qué recelo el fuego airado
> que se prendía por los altos techos;
> qué terror, qué fiereza los rumores,
> .... (p. 34[25])

(How pitiful the shouting of the children;
how tender was the crying of the old;
how horrible the death of strong young men;
how fearful the rage and wild fury
of the cruel and victorious weapons,
of the ferocious and indomitable people;
how confusing the prompt pillage;
the noisy, burning and fierce theft
by the cruel and greedy people;
how frightful, how fearful the wild fire
that was set to the high rooftops,
how terrible, how fierce the rumblings,
...............................)

The Life and Works of Virués

Although I have been unable to duplicate the effect of the initial *k*-sound in the words *qué* and *que* (which begin eight of the twelve lines cited, in addition to the reiterative function in two of the last three lines), as well as in the words *compasión, crueles, confusión, cruel,* and *codiciosa,* the reader can no doubt appreciate the effect of the original and its similarity to the eclogue. Moreover, we need not belabor the parallel in the content of the two selections: suffering and noise are the predominant elements.

If Virués found the horrors of war disquieting, he could also admire compassion in a conqueror. In a verse description of the battle of Tunis (1573), Virués describes what he calls the shameful flight of the Turks who, apparently in fear of the Spanish forces, abandoned the citizens to the "frightful fury of Mars." In contrast, the arrival of John of Austria is "by just and simple amends, / clemency and justice accompanied, / as he makes amicable the inimical band."[26] We may dispute the accuracy of the account,[27] but as we shall see in later chapters, the felicitous conception of a conqueror who befriended the vanquished was to remain a source of inspiration for Virués and would appear in his works in varied guises.

Although we have no picture of Virués, we do possess a self-portrait in verse, if we are to accept the word of Virués's contemporary, the poet Matías de Vargas, whose sonnet, published among the preliminary pages of the *Monserrate,* includes the following lines: "As you at the end of the fifth canto / vividly paint a portrait of yourself...." Upon turning to the corresponding section of the epic poem as directed by Vargas, we read that Virués apparently was

> ...of venerable countenance,
> aquiline nose, lean face,
> pleasant appearance, respectably affable
> with humility and rare modesty;
> pale, blond, comely and of pleasing
> carriage, who gave clear indication,
> by his pleasant appearance, to be a person
> who attests his nobility and Christianity. (Canto 5)

III Virués's Works

The major part of the attention paid to the writings of Virués has concerned itself with his five dramas: *Elisa Dido, La gran Semí-*

ramis (Great Semíramis), *La cruel Casandra* (Cruel Cassandra), *Atila furioso* (Furious Attila), and *La infelice Marcela* (Unhappy Marcela). Although all were composed many years earlier (as Virués himself states in the prologue), they were first published, together with his poems, in the 1609 edition of *Obras trágicas y líricas del Capitán Cristóbal de Virués*.

Generally, most attempts at classification separate *Elisa Dido* from the other four on external evidence: *Elisa Dido* is written in five acts, has a chorus in the Classical tradition, respects the Classical unities of time and place, and seems to conform to a tragic mode. The remaining four dramas are written in three acts, lack a chorus, and appear to depend on death and bloodshed for their classification as tragedies. Others have sensed a more significant contrast between *Unhappy Marcela* and the rest, primarily because it appears to fail as a tragedy. One recent study suggests *Furious Attila* as the atypical play of the group, principally because of its heroine's "equivocal" claim to virility.[28] One obvious conclusion to be drawn, therefore, is that an umbrella classification for the five dramas is inappropriate. Moreover, the varied interpretations with respect to which of the five constitute exceptions to the rest reinforce the need to reexamine not only the plays themselves but the assumptions upon which such judgments have been based. An extreme case is found in the well-known manual by Hurtado and Palencia: after listing the five plays, a summary comment dismisses all but *Elisa Dido*, which is "the least defective of them."[29] No criterion for judging the "defects" is provided, though one may presume that it is related to the adherence (or lack thereof) to the Classical precepts of tragedy. Although the statement is indeed extreme, it should be noted that for many years the Hurtado and Palencia volume was a standard reference work for young scholars in Spain as well as elsewhere.[30] Even the observations of several more cautious scholars, however, share one element in common with the point of departure for the Hurtado and Palencia declaration: a prior assumption about the nature of all five dramas, whereupon deviations from that scheme are looked upon as exceptions or a step backward (or forward, depending upon the prior assumption), or (again depending on the point of departure), as an unusual success or a dismal failure. We shall examine some of these assumptions and their applicability in subsequent chapters, inasmuch as there is a direct relationship between classification and interpretation.

No less varied are the estimates of the chronology of the plays. Moratín is the only one who has gone so far as to attempt a guess about each drama separately. The first, he believes, are *Great Semíramis* and *Cruel Cassandra* (1579); *Furious Attila* would follow (1580) and, curiously, *Unhappy Marcela* and *Elisa Dido* are both assigned to the same year (1581).[31] Although Moratín provides no basis for this hypotheses, Froldi suggests that Sargent's analysis makes Moratín's dates reasonably acceptable.[32] Sargent herself lengthens the period and suggests 1579-90 (but not the "extreme" position of 1570-90 that Hermenegildo mistakenly attributes to her).[33] Others who have concerned themselves with the chronology of the dramas are Mérimée, who postulates 1580-86; Crawford, who suspects 1580-85; and Ruiz Ramón, who suggests the earliest date, 1575-85.[34] Although subsequent critics have learned to be skeptical about Moratín's chronology in general, there is indeed a basis for accepting his judgment that *Semíramis* precedes *Cassandra*, *Attila,* and *Marcela*. As we shall see shortly, it is in the prologue to *Semíramis* that Virués boasts of the novelty of "the first play to be in three acts" (p. 26). Irrespective of the historical validity of this claim, we may safely draw the conclusion that of the four three-act plays, *Semíramis* is chronologically the first.

Without attempting to assign specific dates to particular plays, Sargent does explain that she is "assuming *Dido* to be the first of Virués's plays and *Marcela* the last. This assumption seems to me borne out by the internal evidence of a surer technique and of a gradual moving away from classical limitations...."[35] (We may never know whether there was a typographical error in the transcription of the word "limitations," and whether she meant "imitations" instead. Either word is appropriate, although "limitations" is the more intriguing.)[36] Reasonable as Sargent's hypothesis is, particularly insofar as *Marcela* is concerned, I cannot dispute Froldi's observation in response. Precisely because *Dido* represents what the Italian scholar describes as an intense search quite out of the ordinary, it could belong to any period of Virués's productivity and thus be an isolated episode.[37] We shall have to await discovery of further documentation before we may venture any more precise dates for the composition of the five plays. In the meantime, the consensus of the above-named scholars allows us to consider the late 1570s to the mid 1580s as the period during which Virués composed his dramatic works.

An intriguing puzzle surrounds the date of the *Monserrate*.

Rosell insists that the epic poem was first published in 1588, adding emphatically that it was "not 1587 as Nicolás Antonio and Vicente Ximeno maintain."[38] Accordingly, Juliá and many others have accepted 1588 as the correct date.[39] Mérimée describes the first edition as bearing a title page dated 1588 and a colophon dated 1587, adding that the printing was completed in 1587.[40] A quick glance at Sargent's bibliography gives an apparently equivocal 1587-88, which is explained in an earlier note by a reference to Pérez Pastor, who reported *two* copies, one bearing 1587 and the other 1588 as the date of publication.[41] Sargent then makes a reasonable attempt to reconcile some of the discrepancies by suggesting that a "limited number of copies were run off before the new year, and the title page [may have been] changed for completing the edition before the type was taken down."[42] That this is more than conjectural is supported by the following two accounts.

Martí Grajales describes what in all probability is the same version seen earlier by Mérimée (title page of 1588 and colophon of 1587). However, this is the *second* entry he lists, adding that it differs from the preceding entry only in the date of the title page.[43] This earlier entry has not only the colophon but the title page itself dated 1587. In addition, the *aprobación* is dated September 26, 1586, and the *privilegio* is dated October 18, 1586. The more recent and meticulous investigation of Frank Pierce allows us to put the pieces of the puzzle together. Pierce has taken into account the bibliographies of Nicolás Antonio, Pérez Pastor, Rosell, and others. More importantly, inasmuch as an asterisk next to an entry betokens that Pierce has not seen the item personally, the absence of an asterisk beside the Virués entry assures us of the following facts: there exists an edition of the *Monserrate* dated 1587 in the Biblioteca Nacional de Madrid (thus confirming the data of Martí Grajales), as well as in the British Museum.[44] An edition with the same bibliographical description may be found at the Hispanic Society of America. Consequently, by combining the data of Mérimée, Martí Grajales, and Pierce, together with the plausible explanation of Sargent, we may safely conclude that Virués completed the work in 1586 and that it was first published in December of 1587. This edition continued to be printed well into the following year, thus accounting for a second date, but it remained the *editio princeps*. Not until 1602 was a second edition published and this was, significantly, titled *El Monserrate Segundo*.

IV Virués and His Contemporaries

We have already had occasion to note that well-known writers of his own time included Virués among those whom they saw fit to extol. Cervantes, as we have seen, praises Virués on no fewer than three occasions in works whose publication spans three decades: the pastoral *Galatea* (1585), the novel *Don Quixote* (1605), and the poem *Viaje del Parnaso* (1614). No less significant is the recognition bestowed upon Virués by the man recognized by Cervantes himself as the king of the Spanish *comedia*, Lope de Vega.[45] The more frequently cited reference is the one made to Virués in Lope's *Arte nuevo de hacer comedias en este tiempo* (New Art of Making Plays in This Age): "Captain Virués, a worthy wit, divided [the *comedia*] into three acts, which before had gone on all fours, as on baby's feet, for [*comedias*] were then infants."[46] Lord Holland has rendered this into English couplets:

> Plays of three acts we owe to Virués's pen,
> Which ne'er had crawled but on all fours till then;
> An action suited to that helpless age,
> The infancy of wit, the childhood of the stage.[47]

Ticknor's rendition is at least as felicitous:

> The Captain Virués, a famous wit,
> Cast dramas in three acts, by happy hit;
> For till his time, upon all fours they crept,
> Like helpless babes that never yet had stept.[48]

We may debate, as many have done, whether or not Virués was in fact the first to reduce the genre to three acts, and whether or not Lope de Vega appropriated the formula (and formula it would indeed become) from Virués. With respect to the first point, Virués evidently believed it himself, as he affirms in the prologue to *Great Semíramis,* calling it the first (Spanish) play to be in three acts. That this is not factually accurate may be less significant for an understanding of his art than the fact that he thought of himself as an innovator. As Crawford observes, it is "true that Avendaño's *Comedia Florisea,* in three acts, was printed in 1551, but the Spanish plays with which Virués was acquainted were written in four or rarely five acts, and he had good reasons to believe himself the inventor of a new form."[49]

Did others believe it as well? Once more a curious picture presents itself. Ximeno, citing Virués's own assertion, refers to the reduction in the number of acts as "the glory of having been the first," and quotes Lope's confirmation of "this glory." He then refers to the diarist Diego de Vich (1584–1657) as attributing the innovation to that other Valencian dramatist of the same period, Andrés Rey de Artieda.[50] (The only extant play by Artieda is *Los amantes* [The Lovers], in four acts.) And none other than Cervantes, whose praise of Virués in 1585, 1605, and 1614 reflects familiarity with Virués's works, claimed the distinction for himself in 1615.[51] Yet Lope de Vega, considered by many to be the "creator" of the genre, readily attributes this structural innovation to Virués.

We now enter the realm of conjecture, but it is a rich one. How well did Lope really know the theater of Virués when he wrote his *New Art*? Since Virués's dramas were not published until 1609,[52] we may safely assume that Lope did not have access to a printed version of Virués's plays, particularly not to the *Semíramis* prologue, prior to the composition of the *New Art*.[53] He could very easily have been familiar with one or more of the plays, of course, but this would merely confirm that Virués was one of many who were writing plays in three acts. How did Lope come to believe that Virués was the first?

We do know as a fact that the first laudatory poem in Lope de Vega's *Rimas* (Seville, 1604) is a sonnet by Virués.[54] It would be only natural for Lope to respond in kind and bestow praise on the Valencian. Since there is no contemporary corroboration of the belief that it was indeed Virués who first reduced Spanish *comedias* to three acts, we shall probably never know how Lope came to believe it. The Virués sonnet in Lope's *Rimas* does suggest communication between the two poets. It is not unreasonable to hypothesize some exchange, written or otherwise, in which Virués may have laid claim to his role in the establishment of the three-act formula. That Virués was not disinclined to boast of it is demonstrable; moreover, that Lope would remember that it was for this format that Virués wished to be known is not implausible. Inasmuch as the first known edition of the *New Art* was published together with a new edition of the *Rimas* (Madrid, 1609), Lope had that much more reason to be reminded of Virués as his document was being readied for publication.

That Lope and Virués were personally acquainted is generally accepted as likely, although we possess no documentation. Juana de José Prades suggests the period beginning with Lope's exile to Valencia and ending with another departure by Virués, an interval of more than a decade (1588-1602).[55] The sonnet by Virués praising Lope's poetic talents and published at the head of the latter's collection strengthens the argument. Accordingly, to say that they were acquainted, that the two conversed about poetry and theater (including what they believed to be their own aspirations and achievements) is to describe what in all probability did occur. Far less substantiated is Lope's knowledge of Virués's plays themselves. Morel-Fatio concludes that Lope did not appear to know them at the time he wrote the *New Art*.[56] Juana de José Prades considers this view "totally impossible."[57] However, the basis of her reasoning allows a conclusion that in the period 1605-1608 during which the *New Art* was composed, Lope knew of but was not intimately acquainted with the dramas of Virués.

In 1630 Lope published his *Laurel de Apolo,* cited earlier in our discussion of Virués's biography. Let us look again at the lines which refer to Virués, this time in a slightly larger context:

> In the lovely city which the Turia bathes,
> this funereal and glorious remembrance
> might not suffice to honor Captain Virués.
> Oh unique genius! Rest in peace, you,
> to whom the Comic Muses owed
> the best beginnings they did behold.
> Celebrated tragedies wrote you,
> a sacred Parnassus of *Monserrate* made you,
> writing in wartime all that band,
> taking now sword, now pen, in hand.[58]

Miss José Prades calls forth this praise in support of her belief that "Lope always remembered Virués."[59] Atkinson mentions the reference to Virués and the three-act formula in the *New Art* but goes on to say that "much more significance attaches, however, to his [Lope's] other tribute in *El laurel de Apolo...,* [which] would make of Virués the true founder of the Spanish national drama."[60] I find myself in disagreement with both interpretations.

That Lope praised Virués in 1609 when he published the *New Art* and again in 1630 when he published the *Laurel de Apolo* may in fact reflect that he never forgot the Valencian, but it is surely *post hoc ergo propter hoc* reasoning to cite a 1630 quotation in a discussion of whether or not Lope was well acquainted with Virués's dramas before their publication in 1609. Moreover, the difference in the two references is indeed of a significant substantive order, but the 1630 eulogy does not, as I read it, suggest what Atkinson perceives, namely, the concession that it was Virués who initiated the *comedia* by blending the comic with the tragic. The eulogy can be summarized as follows: first, an introductory four lines (set apart in the original Spanish by a common rhyme pattern of *abab*); second, a couplet (original rhyme of *cc*) to refer to the relationship of the poet and the comic muses; third, a couplet (original rhyme of *dd*) specifying what Virués wrote, namely, tragedies and the *Monserrate;* finally, a couplet (original rhyme of *ee*) describing the soldier-poet. The couplets clearly are the most significant for the matter at hand.

The comic muses represent Lope's reference to the Spanish *comedia.* Lope thus identifies Virués as one of his forerunners, a significant tribute, but no more than that. The second couplet, separated from the preceding one (in the original as well as in my rendition) by a period, does not combine tragic with comic; rather it summarizes Virués's works: tragedies and the *Monserrate.* If this seems obvious, I would respond that such is precisely my point. It is an obvious tribute to a writer who early on contributed to the formation of the *comedia,* whose works are generally viewed as tragedies, and who also wrote the epic *Monserrate.* (Whether or not the dramas are truly tragedies is another matter. The bibliographer Pastor Fuster maintained that Lope's point was specifically to distinguish them from comedies.[61] We could assume the use of the word *tragedias* here to be no more than an echo of the title of Virués's collection, but it is more probably a reflection of Lope's own understanding of the term.)[62] If Lope did really believe that Virués had anticipated him not merely as a writer for the Spanish theater, and not simply in the matter of how many acts constituted a desirable number, but in the intrinsic character of the genre itself, why did he not mention Virués in the *New Art* when he spoke of the delight of variety produced by "tragedy mixed with comedy and Terence with Seneca"?[63]

The conclusion that we may draw from the foregoing is that in the period immediately preceding the publication of the *New Art* in 1609, Lope de Vega knew of Virués (a fact), knew him personally (a likelihood), but aside from Virués's claim to have initiated the three-act format, Lope was not familiar personally with his works

The Life and Works of Virués

(a deduction, based on which elements he attributes and which he does not attribute to Virués in the *New Art*). In contrast, the 1630 eulogy is more than a bibliographical reference. Now Lope knows of Virués's personal life, as is revealed in the reference to the *manner* in which the Valencian wrote: not only does Lope know that Virués was a soldier as well as a poet (not a rarity) but that he composed in battlefield surroundings. Moreover, he knows that the *Monserrate* is not only a poem, but specifically one dealing with a religious theme, and so he is able to say that Virués made of the mountain of Montserrat a "sacred Parnassus." Finally, whatever his own specific definition of *tragedias,* he knew enough in 1630 to use that word and not *comedias* to summarize Virués's dramatic works. In short, what emerges as the most obvious distinction between the two quotations is the more extensive and more intimate knowledge of Virués's works which Lope displays in 1630, a knowledge acquired by Lope de Vega in the years *after* 1609. Perhaps of ultimate significance is the fact that Virués received the most frequent as well as the largest amount of praise in the writings of the two greatest authors of the day. Moreover, the laudatory references by Cervantes and Lope span nearly half a century: from 1585, when Virués was in his thirties, to 1630, when he was no longer living.

CHAPTER 2

The Monserrate

AS the modern-day traveler heads south along the *autopista* which links Barcelona and Valencia, he cannot fail to notice what at first glance appears to be a geological anomaly. Quite unlike any of the numerous mountains that lie in the vicinity, one mount stands dramatically apart for its unique contours as well as for its distinct rocky composition. The traveler is tempted to leave the *autopista* as it passes the Llobregat River, for like a magnet the boulders of the mountain beckon. The innocent visitor will be attracted by his own curiosity in the face of the incomparable phenomenon; the no less impressed but more informed voyager similarly will be drawn in the direction of the towering hulk. As one approaches, the dissimilarity between the awesome rocky mountain and its neighbors becomes more striking and it soon is apparent that the elevation is in reality a small mountain range of its own. (The extension is slightly more than six miles.)[1] The upper region is composed of contiguous vertical pillars or obelisks, a veritable serrated mountain. It is the *monte serrado* called Montserrat.[2]

"Nature and art have made of this mountain a unique marvel," reads the caption on the introductory page of *Legends of Montserrat*.[3] The "art" is revealed in the architecture of the monastery, in the wooden sculpture of the central image of Our Lady of Montserrat and the Christ Child, in the paintings, gems, ceramics, and in the music school of the sanctuary. The magnificent library of the monastery not only attests to the continuing concern of the monks for literary and historiographical pursuits, but reflects as well the legendary themes of which mountain and monastery alike have been the subject.[4] (The library collection includes the 1602 edition of Virués's *Monserrate Segundo*.) It is this aspect of art, namely the poetic blending of fact and legend, that is our concern here. As we shall note, Virués himself is conscious of the blending of "poem and history" in the initial stanza of his work.

I *The Plot of the First Part*

Other than a brief prologue and the twenty numbered cantos, the *Monserrate* has no formal divisions. The separation by parts suggested here has as its basis the structure of the plot, and as its purpose a clearer analysis of the lengthy work. The first three cantos comprise the exordium of the poem. Succinctly stated, this develops as follows: Garín, a pious monk, is deceived by Satan, who tempts him with the flesh of woman. The monk thereupon becomes "guilty of one of the grossest and most atrocious crimes of which human nature is capable," as Ticknor put it in the last century.[5] Recognizing the enormity of his sin, Garín leaves Montserrat and heads penitently for Rome.

A more detailed summary of the first part is as follows: in the initial canto, the poet tells us that he will sing of "that great penitent and pilgrim worthy of poem and history" whose memory is preserved by fame for the glory given to Montserrat. He invokes the muse to aid him in his song and fixes the time of the events as the ninth century ("eight and a half centuries since the day when the Redeemer in human form emerged from Mary's cloister"). Garín, dwelling in a cave on Montserrat, has aroused the wrath of Satan, the latter having considered it a personal injury that a mortal should enjoy the grace and favor of "that Lamb who was and is for me a fierce lion." Satan dispatches two of his subalterns, one of whom disguises himself as a venerable hermit who supposedly has been living in a cave similar to Garín's; the other causes himself to become invisible and possesses the body of the virgin daughter of Don Jofré, count of Barcelona. Jofré is informed that the girl must stay nine days with Garín in his cave. Although the girl recovers immediately following a prayer by Garín (whereupon "Satan flees from the maiden"), Jofré recalls the original condition and insists that his daughter remain with Garín for the full "novena." The canto ends with a description of the girl's loveliness, the final strophe expressing lack of wonder at the eventual defeat of Garín by Satan.

In the second canto, Garín, blinded by the girl's beauty, seeks help by confiding his passion to the "hermit," whose platitudes do not cool his desire. Garín seduces the girl, following which Virués engages in a diatribe on the power of flesh over such figures as Hannibal and Roderick (the king who opened Spain to the invasion of the Moors in 711). Also alluded to but not specifically named are

Samson, David, and Solomon. Amid this array of strength and wisdom, victims of the flesh's ability to "triumph over human knowledge and fortitude," Garín's sin is placed in a context of the eternal human battle of lust versus virtue. The girl joins Garín in tears, wishing for death, but "death does not come to those who call her." The demon-hermit advises Garín to kill the girl in order to keep the matter secret and urges Garín to abandon the mountain. Garín does kill her, recognizes the demon for what he is, and flees in an attempt to hide from the count.

The third canto opens with a dialogue between Garín and his guardian angel, who tells him that he has been defeated by the enemy and that he has sinned shamefully and severely. He warns Garín to make sufficient penance, that before God he has no excuse, and that he should now undertake to "purge your grave sin." Garín accepts the advice, prays to God, confesses his sin but asks: "If you approach man as a severe judge, if you allow pity to be set aside, who can justify himself before you?" Accordingly, he does not ask God for justice but for pity. Pleading for mercy, he promises penitence and vows to go to Rome and seek the favor of the Pope. Sadly abandoning his beloved mountain of Montserrat, Garín heads for the sea and joins General Alberto's Neapolitan armada.

II *The Style of the First Part*

We have already noted, in our introductory chapter, Virués's penchant for repetition. At that time we emphasized his concern for the acoustic effect produced by the repetition of a given sound. Beyond that, we may safely generalize that throughout his works, Virués was conscious of the variegated possibilities inherent in the several types of iteration. In fact, his fondness for iterative devices may be considered one of his weaknesses, for it is so predominant that its abuse at times detracts from its purpose by calling attention to itself.

One of the most common iterative devices is the rhetorical figure known as anaphora, the repetition of a word or words at the beginning of two or more successive verses, clauses, or sentences. Examples may be seen in our previously cited instances in chapter one, for although we stressed the repetition of the initial *sound,* the selections there present as well the iteration of words (*quien* in one instance, *qué* in another, and *quien* once more in the poem cited in note 25 to that chapter). An example occurs in the final strophe of canto 2 of the *Monserrate,* immediately following Garín's murder of the girl and his recognition of the demon as he wishes to flee from the count: *Vuela el sol, vuela el monje* ("[So] flies the sun, [so] flies the monk"). Another instance occurs in the first canto as Satan urges his subalterns to head for Montserrat: *Ya me entendéis, ya veis mis intenciones, / Ya conocéis en lo que estoy resuelto* ("Now you understand me, now you see my intentions, / Now you know what I am resolved to do"). The combination of anaphora here with asyndeton (the omission of conjunctions) creates an effect admired by Classical authors. Defining asyndeton, Longinus cites a passage from the *Odyssey* and observes: "The phrases, disconnected, but none the less rapid, give the impression of an agitation which at the same time checks the utterance and urges it on. And the poet has produced such an effect by his use of asyndeton."[6] Combining the figures produces a cumulative effect of force.[7] In this manner, the poet "preserves the essential character of the repetitions and the asyndeta, and thus too his order is disordered, and similarly his disorder embraces a certain element of order."[8] One could hardly conceive of a more appropriate effect for Satan's words in our poem.

Iteration combined with polyptoton (rhetorical effects gained by change in the grammatical application of a word) is a frequent device and in fact Virués begins the poem with this combination: *La excelsa causa del honor divino / Que causa a Monserrate excelsa gloria* ("The sublime cause of divine honor / Which causes Montserrat sublime glory"). Similarly, the count's description of his tears employs three forms of the verb *hacer* ("to make"): *No os espantéis si destos ojos hago / Ríos, pues las ofensas que a Dios hice / Hacen en el alma de amargura un lago* ("Don't wonder if of these eyes I make / Rivers, for the offenses that to God I made / Make in the soul of bitterness a lake"). Repetition of the same word to produce rhyme is generally frowned upon, but may be permissible when the grammatical function differs. Virués uses this sparingly, and then for dramatic emphasis, as when Garín has exorcised the demon: *De lo que a la doncella maravilla, / El ver en sí la misma maravilla* ("What makes the maiden marvel, / To see in herself the very marvel").

Less artistic but quite extensive is the simple manipulation of the order of words when they are repeated. Again in the first canto we find a typical example, as the poet describes the "divine, heroic, and holy music" which rests upon "heroic, divine, and holy pleasure." This falls somewhat short of the figure known as hyperbaton (the inversion of the normal order), a device not infrequently found in our poem. An example is the convocation of Satan's henchmen in the opening canto: *Valientes capitanes, que a mi lado, / Desde la gran jornada temerosa, / Habéis con tanto esfuerzo militado* ("Brave captains, who at my side, / Since the great fearful battle, / Have with such vigor struggled"). Most of these rhetorical devices can be observed in juxtaposition in the following strophe from canto 2, as Virués attacks lust personified:

Pues cuanto en la milicia heroica y alta,
Donde honor y valor tienen su punto,
Donde sublima, donde fama exalta
Las cosas con excelso contrapunto,
¡Cuánto tú contrapuntas! ¡Cuánta falta
Por ti se tiene, y cuánta sobra! Y junto
¡Cuánto daño y rüina, varios puestos
Trocados por tu mano y contrapuestos!

(For all that in the heroic and lofty militia
Where honor and valor have their place,
Where fame elevates, where it exalts
Things with sublime counterpoint,
How much you counterpoise! How much need
Because of you we have, and how much we don't! And jointly,
How much harm and ruin, various places
Converted by your hand and counterpoised!)

A quick glance at the original strophe above also reveals the versification of the poem: the so-called *octava real* or "regal octave," comprised of strophes of eight hendecasyllabic lines with a rhyme scheme of *abababcc*. In this Virués is following the best of his immediate predecessors: Ercilla's *Araucana* is composed in this meter, as are the Portuguese *Lusiadas* of Camoens (1572) and the Italian *Gerusalemme liberata* of Tasso (1575), as well as the *Orlando furioso* of Ariosto (1516), considered the first to do so.[9] An interesting trait in Virués is the accommodation of the rhyme of the final couplet to suggest antithesis. Some examples are: *enemigo/amigo* (eneny/friend), *punto/contrapunto* (Point/counterpoint), *Cordero/fiero* (Lamb [=Christ]/wild), *santamente/en saña ardiente* (in a saintly manner/in burning anger), *defensas/ofensas* (defenses/offenses), *fuego/sosiego* (fire/calm), *flaqueza/fortaleza* (weakness/fortitude), and many more. As can bee seen from the nature of the foregoing examples, the type of antithesis is directly related to the content of the poem. Indeed, we might well consider them as a guide to the development of the plot. The first canto, for example, as it ends with the warning that we should not wonder that Garín will lose the battle with Satan, significantly concludes with the rhyme of *belleza/flaqueza (beauty/* weakness). No less meaningful — hence we should not dismiss it too hastily as poor poetry — is the use on three separate occasions in canto 3 (the canto of the seduction and homicide of the rhyme *culpa/disculpa* (sin/exculpation).

The above should not be taken to mean that the final couplet is consistently used to reflect the antithetical nature of the content. The rhyme may in fact be employed to reinforce an affinity between two concepts. Examples include *victoria/gloria* (victory/glory), *pío/fío* (pious/trust), *impaciente/ardiente* (impatient/ardent), *pena/condena* (suffering/condemns, and *cadena/ pena* chain/suffering). This series of examples, together with the preceding set, helps us to appreciate Virués use of the rhyme of the final couplet to point up the inner significance of the poetic narrative. As in the thrice-stated sin/exculpation antithesis, so in the pairs of similar concepts do we find a greater significance than a coincidence of acoustic rhyme. As the girl is left alone with Garín toward the close of the first canto, three couplets which on first reading reflect synonymous content in fact warn us of the danger. Twice a strophe concludes with *doncella/ella* (maiden/she), and once more with *bella/doncella* (beautiful/maiden). As we learn from the ensuing plot, these similar lexical elements actually reveal danger inherent in leaving a beautiful virgin alone with a man in the circumstances our poem describes. Yet another instance of apparently similar concepts used to convey conflicting ideas is found in Satan's lament: "I must suffer the great rigor of heaven / Without there being for me ever consolation," in which the rhyme of *cielo/consuelo* (heaven/-consolation) is seen to reveal the devil's conflict.

III *The Ambience of the First Part*

Particularly as we embark upon the analysis of a work with an obvious religious orientation, it is tempting to see three levels of interpretation. Indeed, we may legitimately insist that celestial, terrestrial, and infernal levels have already been introduced. Virués himself was forced to face the problem of composing a Christian work within a Classical or pagan framework. Let us read with special care the second strophe of the poem, which at first glance seems to be no more than the conventional invocation to the poetic muse:

> You, holy muse, who as reward offers
> Divine laurel wreath from your hand to
> The same person whom you endow and enrich
> By your grace of sovereign intent,
> For by that you enlighten and exalt
> With divine favor human style,
> Raise now my voice to such extent
> That heroic be my second chant.

When we recall how the Classical authors depicted Calliope, muse of heroic verse, we recognize a number of features: "She was represented with an epic poem in one hand and a trumpet in the other, and generally crowned with laurel."[10] Virués's solution, as our note indicates, was not unlike that of many another Christian composer of heroic poetry: the muse remains anonymous, retains her Classical properties, yet is readily merged with the qualities of a Christian providence.[11] (That Virués was aware of the problem presented to the poet who wished to emulate Virgil while praising the Virgin is clear from the prologue, which we shall discuss at a later stage in this volume.)

The duality which is evident in the poet's approach to his material — Christian topic and ethic, within pagan literary conventions — has its counterpart in the tale itself. The *Monserrate* is at once the story of a particular set of persons and a Christian allegory. Our summary of the first three cantos provides an outline of the former; an analysis of selected elements will clarify the latter.

How may we reach the conclusion that Virués has composed an allegorical poem? We must first arrive at an arbitrary agreement on the meaning of allegory, and arbitrary it must be as anyone who is familiar with the term will admit.[12] We shall use it here in its least complex definition, namely the depiction of general truths as narrated through individual characters and events whose literal meanings reveal a cosmological significance. We must not, however, seek allegory in every line of the poem. No less an authority than Tasso himself has sounded the warning: "Without denigrating the importance of either a cosmology of correspondence or a poetic of correspondence, we have assurance from Torquato Tasso himself that there is no such thing as an allegory in which there is correspondence 'in every particle.' "[13] Virués understood this well, so that the opening strophe of the *Monserrate* has particular relevance for our concern. The poet tells that he will sing of "that great penitent and pilgrim worthy of poem and history."

To a large extent this is a reference to Aristotle's *Poetics* and the well-known principle of the particular and the universal truths: "Thus the difference between the historian and the poet is not in their utterances being in verse or prose ... [but] in the fact that the historian speaks of what has happened, the poet of the kind of thing that *can* happen. Hence also poetry is a more philosophical and serious business than history; for poetry speaks more of universals, history of particulars."[14] The significance of Virués's words "poem and history" lies not merely in his recognition of the importance of Aristotle (whom he cites in the prologue), but in the announcement that the poet will sing the truth of *both* the universal and the particular. He will recount a legend whose major elements are known (the particulars) and portray them in a poetic ambience which is no less true in the Aristotelian sense (the universals). Moreover, although he is telling the story of Garín's sin (the particular), he explains that transgression as the result of "*our* mortal weakness" (the universal).[15] Similarly, although he fixes the time of the events in a most prosaic manner (mid-ninth century, as the historico-legendary background demands), the particular time is related to another particular time, but one with transcendental significance: "eight and a half centuries since the day when the Redeemer in human form emerged from Mary's cloister." A parallel frame of reference is found in Satan's convocation of his subalterns, whom he describes as having been at his side "since the great fearful battle." Further references to Satan as "king of Tartarus," as well as allusions to Acheron, Cocytus, Phlegethon, and Lethe,[16] also serve a purpose more significant than the fusion of Christian and pagan beliefs. The repeated juxtaposition of geographical references to Montserrat and its environs with mythological topography not only continues the particular-universal antithesis but reinforces the dualistic ambience of the poem, namely, that the events narrated which occur to Garín have an allegorical application. Satan could hardly be clearer on this point than when he describes Montserrat as causing him no less torment than Calvary or Carmel.

We have spoken of a dualistic ambience. It would, of course, be convenient to speak of *three* levels in a religious poem, and we could begin with the tripartite stratification of heaven and hell framing the world of mortal man. However, although we can see significance in various numbers and their combinations,[17] what emerges in the material we are studying is a persistent duality. In this respect we can find relevance to our poem in the symbolism of the number two, which "stands for echo, reflection, conflict and counterpoise or contraposition...; it also corresponds to the passage of time — the line which goes from behind forward.... It is also symbolic of the first nucleus of matter, of nature in opposition to the creator, of the moon as opposed to the sun.... [Two] connotes shadow and the bisexuality of all things, or dualism (represented by the basic myth of the Gemini) in the sense of the connecting link between the immortal and the mortal...."[18] This dualism is found in the characters as well.

IV *The Characters of the First Part*

Despite the foregoing, we need not place undue emphasis on any symbolism inherent in the number two. We must simply bear in mind the fundamental duality with which Virués represents the world of the *Monserrate*. Thus far we have observed a twofold nature in the style and in the ambience. As we examine the characters of the first part, we note a persistent tendency to portray them in a dualistic fashion even as we may sense a triadic representation. (In this respect, as in so many others, we can readily observe a parallel with Genesis: God creates man and a fundamental dualism is established. By creating woman an apparent triad is created, yet the tendency is ever to make twosomes: God and human, rather than God, man, and woman; Adam and Eve, when confronted by the serpent, are separated into serpent and Eve, then Eve and Adam, then Adam and God, then Adam and Eve as one pair, and God and the serpent as another. Even the tree represents the knowledge of two antithetical concepts, the result of which is Cain as well as Abel, the former being called to account by God for his failure to keep the brotherhood.)

As we observe the character of the devil in the *Monserrate*, we may easily discern a parody of the Holy Trinity, for in Satan, in the subaltern who assumes the guise of a monk, and in the subaltern who possesses the body of the girl, we have a ready analogue of Father, Son, and Holy Ghost. Yet the treatment of these demonic figures in the poems inhibits such an interpretation (although it does not forbid the simple analogy).[19] From the very beginning, Virués presents the devil in some manner of bilateral opposition. First with Garín, as the two are introduced in the same strophe of the first canto, it is expressly stated that it is Garín's saintliness that has moved the demon to fury. This in itself is replete with significance, for it places into conflict Garín and Satan in all their conceivable representations: saint and devil, good and evil, man and demon. Most intriguing, perhaps, is what motivates Satan: the human vice of envy, and it is man whom he envies, "considering his [Garín's] virtue as a personal insult." Thus although the devil appears to be placed in opposition to man, he is shown to have human vices and therefore to have both supernatural and human traits. Here is how he himself describes his envy of man's good fortune:

> That I should be the one of eternal crying!
> And man so truly now is trying
> With the grace and favor of that Lamb
> Who was and is for me fierce lion!
> That a vile creature, dull, and full
> Of misfortunes and imperfections
> . . . .
> Should inherit that pleasant domain
> Which has its seat over Septentrion,[20]
> That sweet, rich and to me native terrain,
> Full of eternal joy and halcyon! (Canto 1)

Satan goes on to express his rage at having been deprived of his wealth by heaven, which "like a father" favors man. Since the primeval day when Satan lost his heavenly status his arm is no longer strong enough to wage war upon heaven. Therefore he avenges himself upon man. In this way, narrates Virués, "the wild king of terrible Tartarus provokes himself; thus he with angry envy suffers his misfortune," It is at this point that he convokes his lieutenants.

Of all the sins none is more inherently divisive than envy.[21] It is, of course, the source of Cain's transgression. The parallel with Genesis continues, therefore, as the devil, envious because God favors man, considers himself in opposition to man. But he "provokes himself," says Virués, and consequently produces a bifurcated demon: a visible self and an invisible self. (In accordance with our earlier observations on the rhyme of final couplets, the present analysis reinforces the supposition that what may appear to be poor poetry finds its more significant purpose in underscoring a similarity or antithesis or, in the present instance, a reduplication: "To Barcelona the one goes invisible; / The mount the other reaches and goes visible.") Even the physical locations will continue the dualism, for Garín, residing in his cave, will be the object of the two demons' efforts to be brought "here to my infernal eternal cave," as Satan instructs. Moreover, the devil himself describes his envy of "the glory which this monk attains" as the cause of his "mortal immortal anxiety."

If Satan functions on an ambivalent level of infernal-mortal, so too Garín is presented as a composite of mortal and saintly qualities. Virués introduces him to us as having his "spirit lit up in saintliness," and in the very next line calls him "the great man." In fact, Virués tends to emphasize his saintly attributes ("subjecting his body and soul to trial / Of almost more than human and mortal man [would]"), whereas Satan harps on Garín's status as a mere man formed of dust ("vile" being a favorite adjective to describe the monk). There exists, then, an interesting parallel of devil and man, each appropriating some characteristics of the creature hierarchically above him.[22] The dramatic tension of the *Monserrate* will frequently turn on the duality inherent in Garín. "Man is made of two natures," says the Italian humanist Giovanni-Battista Gelli in his *La Circe* (1549), "one corporeal and terrestrial, the other divine and celestial; in the one he resembles beasts, in the other those immaterial substances which turn the heavens."[23]

No need exists, of course, to stress the duality, or more specifically, the duplicity of each of the two demons dispatched by Satan. One assumes the guise of a holy monk; the other inhabits the body of a young virgin. And once more a reduplication is established as each disguised demon sets about to deceive a man: Garín and Jofré, respectively. As for the girl, Virués portrays her in a fashion which, were we to limit our reading to what we have called the first part of the poem, we would most likely call a weak characterization. The major portion of those lines which depict her are limited to extolling her physical beauty. Yet we cannot say that she personifies beauty, for she seems to have no will of her own. Her function appears to be quite passive, from the possession (in the spiritual sense) of her body by the demon to the possession (in the physical sense) of her body by the monk. What is more, she is the only character in this part of the poem who remains anonymous.[24] On the other hand, Virués lays the groundwork for the final part of the poem as he describes, in the opening canto, the girl's reaction to finding herself on the mountain after Garín had exorcised the demon. According to the poet, her reaction was not unlike that of Lazarus raised from the dead. For the reader familiar with the legend of Montserrat, the analogy is a clear one, and we shall return to it as we study the concluding part of the poem. For the moment, however, it is important to note that although a certain polarization exists in the person of the girl — she is in turn the count's daughter, the body possessed by the demon, or the victim of Garín — she is always portrayed as a passive individual. If we have gradually become accustomed to a dualistic presentation of characters in the *Monserrate*, the characterization of the girl seems then to lack its corresponding complement. Despite her death — even if we did not know the eventual culmination of the legend — we are left with a sensation that her character has remained uninished. In view of the ultimate outcome, we may conclude that this effect was intentional on the part of the poet.

V *Exile*

We have alluded to the evident parallels between the first part of the *Monserrate* and the initial chapters of Genesis. This is, of course, not happenstance but a confirmation of the essential nature of Virués's poem. Garín's transgression combines those of Adam and Cain: the tasting of forbidden fruit at the instigation of the devil, followed by homicide. The reaction in each case is similar as well: a desire to flee, followed by the recognition that flight from God is impossible. There is a note of irony in the biblical account that is supplanted in the Virués poem in accordance with a Christian awareness. The omnipotent God of Genesis apparently must seek out the transgressor: "Adam and his wife hid themselves from the presence of the Lord God amongst the trees of the garden. And the Lord God called unto Adam, and said unto him, Where art thou?"[25] Garín, aware that nothing can be hidden from God, relates his desire for concealment to the fear of *human* vengeance and tries to hide from the count. As for God, Garín begins his confessional prayer by admitting to having sinned "in thy royal presence" (canto 3).

As we noted earlier, Garín rejects the concept of a vengeful judge as his God, believing instead in a God of mercy. Unlike Adam or Cain, Garín does not engage God in dialogue. His words remain unanswered as he promises to do penance, linking his transgression to the original sin. In this Garín — or more accurately, Virués — is adhering to the doctrine expounded by the Council of Trent: "If anyone asserts that the disobedience of Adam injured only himself and not his offspring..., let him be anathema."[26] Garín similarly expresses Catholic dogma as he recognizes his God-given ability to choose between good and evil and that it is his own weakness that is at fault:

> For you, Lord, who with your occult science
> My soul with a certain light alit,
> Giving my will free reign enough
> With which the enemy to resist
> You show me, since resistance I'd not enough
> That 'tis not right that words I waste
> On false excuse in order me to save
> Which only would increase my sins so grave.
> (Canto 3)

It was at the Council of Trent as well that the proposition that "man's free will has been wholly lost and destroyed after Adam's sin" was anathematized. Similarly judged anathema was the proposition that "it is not in the power of man to make his ways evil, but that evil works as well as good are wrought by God ... so that the betrayal of Judas is no less his work than the calling of Paul."[27] In short, whereas Adam's transgression conferred a state of sin upon all humans, the partaking of the tree of the knowledge of good and evil deprived man of the innocence of that knowledge. Accordingly, man cannot avoid the choice, and conversely, that choice will be man's to make.

Because the God of the Christian era is much less a vengeful one than that of Genesis, he is less likely to exact punishment and, through Christ, more likely to inspire penitence and penance. Accordingly, the Council of Trent also anathematized the proposition that "penance is not truly and properly a sacrament in the Catholic Church, instituted for the faithful by Christ our Lord, for their reconciliation to God whenever they fall into sin after baptism."[28] Also declared anathema was the proposition that "for entire and perfect remission of sins three acts are not required in a penitent, to be as it were the matter of the sacrament, namely contrition, confession and satisfaction."[20] This helps to clarify the words of the guardian angel to Garín in the third canto: "Weep and do sufficient penance: / ... / Go now to purge your grave sin."

In Genesis, God is not satisfied with contrition (which is implicit in the attempt to hide from God) and immediately imposes punishment: Eve will suffer pain in childbirth, Adam will have to endure sweat and toil through thorns and thistles before he can reap food from the ground, and both Adam and Eve are driven from Eden. In the *Monserrate,* Garín confesses the enormity of his sin, describes his "contrite and humbled heart," and himself promises:

> I shall give you with rare penitence,
> With signs and weeping of bitterness,
> With pain that will my spirit renew
> What a contrite heart owes to you.   (Canto 3)

Thus it is not God but the sinner who exiles himself from Montserrat, ironically accepting the suggestion made earlier by the demon disguised as the monk ("he should kill that woman and bury her, / and then from the mount exile himself"). The theme of exile, of being removed from one's accustomed habitat, represents the first punishment imposed upon man. The literature relating to that theme is a vast one and is beyond the scope of the present study. What is to the point here, however, is that in our poem, whose first three cantos we have considered as an analogue of the early chapters of Genesis, the sin of the monk of Montserrat gives rise to the same punishment as that imposed upon Adam and Eve — sent forth from Eden — and upon Cain: "a fugitive and a vagabond shalt thou be in the earth" (Genesis, 4:12). The exile of Garín from Montserrat converts him from a hermit figure to a wanderer. Thus in content and in structure, Virués has fused the biblical and the epic. This brings us to the peregrination of Garín and what we may call the second part of the *Monserrate.*

VI   *Transition*

In his careful but brief analysis of the *Monserrate,* Pierce observes that the entire central portion of the poem — Garín's adventures on the voyage to Rome — could be passed over without harm to the principal action.[30] If the main action must be confined to the legend of the monastery on the mountain, we might agree that a voyage to Italy can be of only tangential significance. However, despite its title, the *Monserrate* is not limited to a poetic account of the historico-legendary events connected with the founding of the monastery. What Pierce has called the "central part" of the poem — by which he evidently has in mind the structure (cantos 4-15) and not the sense — is not a digression if we are to accept this work as part of the epic tradition.

Canto 4 does indeed give the impression that a new phase has begun. The transition appears to be the opening-line comment that Garín had finished the prayers described in the last strophe of the preceding canto. As the monk gazes about him and sees the sculptured representations of great battles of history with which the ship is decorated, the poet leaves the ninth-century events in order to praise the accomplishments of the battle of Lepanto, which Virués contrasts with the (to him) less significant Roman, Persian, and Greek victories of antiquity. We seem to have lost the thread of the narrative, yet there is a new transition as the poet recites the word "peregrine,"[31] which is immediately followed by the line "worthy of poem and history." We have come upon this line before: it is the exact wording of the fourth line of the opening canto. What is more, the parallel does not end here. Let us compare the initial strophe of the poem with the strophe in question; in canto 1:

> *La excelsa causa del honor divino*
> *Que causa a Monserrate excelsa gloria,*
> *Y aquel gran penitente y peregrino*
> *De poema dignísimo y de historia,*
> *Del cual allí por celestial camino*
> *Hace la fama singular memoria ...*

> (The sublime cause of divine honor
> Which causes Montserrat sublime glory,
> And that great penitent and [pilgrim] peregrine
> Worthy of poem and history,
> Of whom along celestial lines
> Fame makes unique memory ...)

and in canto 4:

> *Así sea, señor, así el divino*
> *Os lo conceda, cuanto a su alta gloria*

The Monserrate

> *Sea conveniente, en su real camino*
> *No discrepando un punto la memoria:*
> *Así seáis, en modo peregrino,*
> *De poema dignísimo y de historia...*

(May it be so, sire,[32] may thus the [Lord] divine
grant you all that to his high glory
Fitting be, along its regal line
Not straying one iota in its memory:
So be you, in ways so peregrine,
Worthy of poem and history...)

There is no need to comment upon the evident echo of the poem's beginning. Its function here is to relate the events of the apparent digression — ancient and future glories — to the adventures of Garín. This in turn provides an atmosphere that reinforces two facets of the poem. One is the reaffirmation of the relationship between particulars and universals. The other is a characteristic of the epic genre which would be missing were we to read the poem as exclusively the story of events relating to the founding of the monastery. I refer to the principle known as *in medias res,* a convention which provides that epic poets begin their tale in the "middle of the thing," as Horace suggested: "[The poet] plunges his hearer into the middle of the story as if it were already familiar to him ... Moreover, so inventive is he, and so skillfully does he blend fact and fiction, that the middle is not inconsistent with the beginning, nor the end with the middle."[33]

The anachronistic device of having the poet complement Garín's review in the ninth century of ancient military battles by narrating the glories of the sixteenth-century battle of Lepanto forces the reader to contemplate the events of the *Monserrate* with a more universal perspective. We are in the middle of man's evolving history. Even within the particular story of Garín, however, we have begun *in medias res.* This would not be so if we were to read the poem as being exclusively about Montserrat, for in that event we could safely state that the temptation of the monk and the seduction and murder of the girl constitute the beginning of that story. As Virués narrates the second part of the poem, he not only sets up an *in medias res* structure in the larger sense as noted above, but reminds us that we have come upon Garín in the middle of *his* life as well. As the narrative returns to the affairs of the monk by means of the evocative strophe cited above, Garín reveals for the first time that his given name is Juan, that at the age of one he had been floating in a cockleshell after a storm, the shell having deposited him on the beach of an island at the mouth of the Llobregat River (near Barcelona), and that an old man had cared for him and subsequently taken him to Montserrat when Garín reached the age of six.[34]

In canto 5 we are told that the old man lived twenty years with Garín and that since his death another twenty have passed, during which Garín has lived alone in Montserrat. It is not made clear whether the first group of twenty years included the earlier period on the island or whether those twenty refer only to the time spent after moving on to Montserrat. In any event, the data given in the fifth canto place Garín's age at the time of the events being narrated as somewhere in his early to middle forties. This information reinforces the *in medias res* effect in yet another sense. Singleton observes about the opening line of Dante's *Inferno* that "midway in the journey of our life" places the poet's age at thirty-five and quotes Psalm 90 to the effect that the biblical "life span of seventy years had become a part of accepted medical and philosophical opinion."[35] The verse in Psalm 90 to which Singleton refers goes on, however: "The days of our years are threescore years and ten; and if by reason of strength they be fourscore years, yet is their strength labor and sorrow...." In other words, we need not be categorical about the human life span; we may accept a broader spread and, in fact, the biblical statement seems to urge us not to be specific. Garín's age, then, is quite literally middle age.

The narration of Garín's provenance in canto 4 and the continuation of his story (including a magnificent description of Montserrat, the etymology of the mountain's name, and the reference to the monk's age) is interrupted by shouts of "Man overboard! Man overboard!" The incident is rapid and seems to have no bearing upon the main narrative. However, it serves two complementary purposes. On a structural level, it interrupts the account of the principal character's tale, thus evading potential monotony and creating some measure of suspense. On the allegorical level, the image of the man lost at sea reinforces the pilgrim's narrative of his own peregrinations, first shortly after birth, and now once more in his middle years.

The revelation that Garín had arrived floating in a vessel in the sea has a significance that is not easily missed but which would be sorely lacking if we were to consider this portion of the poem as extraneous to the main plot. The epic which Virués proposed to write has, until this second part, failed to provide us with an understanding that the protagonist is endowed with the traditional characteristics of the hero. If the specific identification of the vessel as a cockleshell reinforces the allegorical role of the pilgrim and wanderer, the general notion of having arrived in this fashion readily accommodates the archetypal conception of the birth of the hero. Moses springs to mind, but perhaps a closer parallel is found in the legendary account of Pope Gregory I:

Pope Gregory the Great (A.D. 540?-604) was born of noble twins who at the instigation of the devil had committed incest. His penitent mother set him to sea in a little casket. He was found and fostered by fishermen, and at the age of six was sent to a cloister to be educated as a priest. But he desired the life of a knightly warrior. Entering a boat, he was borne miraculously to the country of his parents, where he won the hand of the queen — who presently proved to be his mother. After discovery of this second incest, Gregory remained seventeen years in penance, chained to a rock in the middle of the sea. The keys to the chains were tossed to the waters, but when at the end of the long period they were discovered in the belly of a fish, this was taken to be a providential sign: the penitent was conducted to Rome, where in due course he was elected Pope.[36]

We can now see added significance in Garín's earlier acknowledgment that God had provided him with sufficient freedom of will to have been able to resist the temptation. Without the power to determine the course of his actions, Garín could not be viewed as a hero. "The tragic hero rises above the common ruck by the very fact of his purpose, even when it is a guilty one.... Many works deal entirely or principally with victims. They repeat in one way or another the theme expressed by Gloucester in *King Lear:* 'As flies to wanton boys are we to the gods; / They kill us for their sport.' This theme of uncontrollable fatality is probably older ... than that of tragedy. It is illustrated by a whole period, the medieval, in which it was thought to be the very essence of tragedy."[37]

The early cantos of the second part of the *Monserrate,* then, provide us with some essential ingredients without which we could not continue. Moreover, the structure is one which provides the transition in a weaving and pitching fashion not unlike the motion of the sea. If earlier we thought that we had started at the beginning, we have now come to realize that as we progress further forward in time we learn more of what had occurred prior to the apparent beginning. And inasmuch as even that beginning has a prior history (Garín's parentage, his birth, and his first year of life), the diversions in the main narrative begin to reveal their relevance to the larger poem.

Auerbach, after citing correspondence between Goethe and Schiller with respect to the element of suspense in Homer, comments: "The 'retarding element,' the 'going back and forth' by means of episodes, seems to me, too, in the Homeric poems, to be opposed to any tensional and suspensive striving toward a goal, and doubtless Schiller is right in regard to Homer when he says that what he gives us is 'simply the quiet existence and operation of things in accordance with their natures'; Homer's goal 'is already present in every point of his progress.' "[38] Accordingly, by means of the structure of the *Monserrate,* as well as by the gradual mythification of the hero, we are led to comprehend the nature of the poem. That the protagonist, in order to be heroic, must be endowed with the ability to choose, is implicit in the above-quoted definition by Mandel. The attribute of volition has also been discussed in a theological context as reinforced by the Council of Trent. As we shall see in our chapter on fortune and free will in Virués's dramatic works, the subject is a fundamental one for the understanding of his theater. With respect to the matter at hand, we note once more a fusion of religious and Classical motifs.

Aristotle had defined three categories as the faculties of the soul: intellect, will, and memory. Moreover, throughout the *Poetics* there runs a commentary on the kinds of recognition scenes. Virués evidently considered the faculty of will related to the revelation of identity. In this he is perhaps confusing his readings of Aristotle, but it is of significance that in the *Monserrate* this concept appears a decade earlier than in a theoretical treatment of the matter in the famous treatise *Philosophía antigua poética* of Alonso López Pinciano, published in 1596. In one of the dialogues from this work, a comment is made on Heliodorus's *Ethiopian History:* "And although in its form the recognition belongs to the category of the least artistic recognitions, which is that of will...," into which Forcione interjects the following observation: "El Pinciano reinterprets Aristotle's discussion of recognition to fit into the three categories of *intellect, will,* and *memory;* his recognition by will is a modification of Aristotle's second category and includes all those recognitions in which a character deliberately reveals his identity."[39] Like Pinciano, Virués merges the faculty of will with the

The Monserrate

revelation of identity. In the *Monserrate,* this combination may be due less to an original interpretation of Aristotle than to the nature of the poem itself. In the admixture of religious and Classical motifs — particularly in the post-Tridentine period — the concomitant need to relate philosophical free will to literary recognition may very well have been inherent in the kind of work Virués was attempting to create.[40]

VII   *Fortune and the Hero*

If the foregoing has itself seemed to be a digression, the parenthesis has enabled us to continue the reading of our poem with a clearer understanding of its hero, its ideological base, and its literary structure. The structure, as we have observed, has a characteristic to-and-fro weaving. In addition to the points raised above, this trait requires us to look backward as we move forward, so that matters which may have appeared to be of only passing interest on first reading assume a larger importance as subsequent elements tie them together. Before proceeding with the second part of the *Monserrate,* it will be to our advantage to connect, however briefly, the dualistic style which we noted in the first part and the two major kinds of fortune which are at work. To do justice to the latter would be far beyond the scope of the present study. A succinct consideration of the subject, however, is not only relevant but fundamental for our comprehension of the poem in general and the trials of the hero in particular.

Although the literature on the subject is so vast that even a bibliography of the major works on fortune is beyond our capabilities here, we can readily grasp the basic dichotomy by turning to the concise presentation of Otis Green, who explains that "in the final analysis ... there are but two Fortunes: what I have elsewhere called *Fortuna de tejas arriba* and *Fortuna de tejas abajo* —Fortune above and Fortune below the roof tiles.[41] The first is in the final analysis equated with God's will.... The second is a personification of the disorder, the vicissitudes, the ups and downs of human life, equated with human prudence during the up periods and with human stupidity or passionate willfulness during the down periods."[42] In subsequent passages, Green further simplifies the distinction by contrasting the two "conceptions of Fortune, as symbol either of Providence or of simple contingency,"[43] and by differentiating between "Christian Fortune, a minister who carries out the divine providence," and "worldly Fortune, the symbol of mutability."[44]

Clarified — and only to a limited extent oversimplified — in this manner, this additional duality may now be related to the *Monserrate*.[45] The revelation at the beginning of the second part that Garín arrived in a cockleshell and survived a seastorm does more than satisfy the exigencies of the *in medias res* formula as it endows the protagonist with attributes of the mythical hero. The particular manner chosen — survival by means of nature despite a storm caused by nature — suggests as well the intervention of providence.[46] Of this we have no knowledge until canto 4. Our initial encounter with Garín showed us a man tempted by the flesh (albeit at the instigation of the devil) who chose to yield to that temptation and, furthermore, willingly committed murder. In short, as he himself recognizes, a man endowed with will.

The temptation, it will be recalled, has consistently been represented in the guise of something good. Satan has presented himself as a fellow hermit or within the body of a beautiful maiden. The analogy with Genesis must not be forgotten: the serpent appeared *prior* to the fall of man and *within* the confines of Eden. In other words, even in Paradise — prototype in time and place of goodness itself — the serpent lurked ready to lead man to perdition, which is to say that the devil made his first appearance in the garden planted by God (Genesis, 2:8), which, along with everything else created by God "was very good" (1:31). In canto 5, Garín is once more confronted by Satan in a holy place even as the monk attempts to worship "with devout intent." The ever-present dualism assumes a dramatic tone as an angel of God replaces the demonic vision. The encouragement by the angel reinforces the concept of man's will:

> Rise, don't swoon, and persevere,
> Try, don't give in, take heart,
> Go more encouraged in your career;
> Have faith, go on with what you first did start.
> As plain you see I come from the sublime sphere,
> Where you can earn eternal hearth;
> Do not believe the illusions just past,
> God hears hearts that are contrite and fast.
>
> (Canto 5)

Garín's position is quite unlike that of Gloucester in *King Lear* ("As flies to wanton boys are we to the gods; / They kill us for their sport"). If Garín is in some senses the toy of God and Satan, he is nonetheless endowed with the ability to choose between them and earn the appropriate reward. That this paradox is a reflection of the times is the thesis of some modern scholars. Trinkaus cites William Bouwsma's *Venice and the Defense of Republican Liberty* (1968) with respect to the "struggle between 'medieval' and 'Renaissance' political and cultural values not only in Bruni's Florence and Sarpi's Venice but more generally between the Catholic Counter-Reformation and Renaissance republicanism broadly conceived.... Corresponding to the historicist and philosophically skeptical character of humanism, he believes, a new kind of Christian vision emerges, one which simultaneously stresses the primacy of the will and salvation by grace."[47]

This simultaneity is, of course, another aspect of the dualistic nature of the poem that we have noted earlier. On the ideological level, the encounter in canto 5 with first a demonic and then an angelic manifestation underscores not only the primacy of will as a concomitant of grace (rather than in opposition to it), but reveals the fallacy of the "wheel of fortune" metaphor. The angel, as quoted above, has stressed the attainability of heaven through the grace of God for those who have stout hearts and who persevere. This was intended to refute the reasoning of the demon's argument moments earlier. Satan had ridiculed Garín's efforts to seek consolation: "There is no seat for you in paradise." The devil, claiming to be God's messenger, tells Garín that the sentence condemning him to the eternal flames is irrevocable but that while he retains his mortal life, fortune will be a friend and spin with him. This he may attain through his good works, says the demon, while hell will be the result of his bad ones. Insofar as the devil's argument is "right" or "wrong," a Christian point of view contrasting angel and demon — which is to say, good and evil — makes of the devil's assertion simply a falsehood. The fallacy — and herein lies our interest — consists of the confusion of the two kinds of fortune discussed earlier. Satan is portraying what Green has called "Christian Fortune, a minister who carries out the divine providence," while in fact adhering to the attributes of "worldly Fortune, the symbol of mutability." The distinction, it goes without saying, was characteristic of the age; the confusion could, as in the works of Virués, be employed to point out that despite the vicissitudes of quotidian life, the will and the resultant behavior of the individual — rather than fate or fortune — determined a large measure of the ultimate outcome.

The above seems clearer in the poem we are discussing than in the theater of Virués. What makes it so readily apparent in the fifth canto of the *Monserrate* is not only that the reader is presented with the opposing views of a devil and an angel but that the episode in question takes place at the shrine of Mary Magdalene, prototype of the sinner turned saint through faith and repentance; that is, will nurtured by grace. That Garín comprehends that bilateral aspect is underscored by the closing lines of his prayer to God following the vision of the angel: "You open unto [this poor pilgrim] the wide portal of your grace; / You want him, Lord, to go on living and convert." What more appropriate place for this realization than the shrine of Mary Magdalene? Accordingly, more than the mere passage of time is conveyed by the opening lines of canto 7, which compare Garín's arrival at the shrine ("dark night") with his departure ("clear day"). The imagery is similar to that found in the Middle English lyric, "Maiden in the Mor Lay," which finds its origins in "the transmission of [the] ballad of a saint from the south of France or Catalonia to northern Europe...."[48] In the English lyric, as Harris points out, the "structure of the [first] stanza builds to a climax with the last word, 'day,' and 'day' comes with the force of an epiphany.... Christ, as the Light of the World, is, of course, often figured forth as the Day, but the night/day imagery also has broader connotations.... In wider religious contexts it suggests the rhythm of penance and forgiveness as well as the historical coming of Christ after the 'dark ages.'"[49] The parallel with the imagery and context of the *Monserrate* is patent.

VIII *Purposeful Intrusion*

Earlier we noted the diatribe on lust in canto 2. The author, on such occasions, interrupts the narrative and makes his presence felt. On that first occasion, Virués addressed lust personified, and began the digression by including himself with *us*. That is to say, not only did the poet engage in a sermon; he reinforced as well the allegorical tone begun in the first canto by speaking of *our* mortal weakness. An interesting variation of the narrator's intrusion is to be found in canto 2, following the seduction but prior to the murder. The narrator actually attempts to speak to his character in an endeavor to warn him away from further transgression:

The Monserrate 55

> Where are you going, Garín? Stop, don't go;
> Protect yourself from greater trouble:
> Don't let pain blind you; watch that you don't fall
> Into another river of a greater current:
> Watch out that after you have taken counsel
> From the cruel deadly serpent
> Whom you take for a saintly friend and aid,
> There not arise a greater cascade.   (Canto 2)[50]

In canto 7, another interruption by the poet provides a new variation. This time Virués addresses man. The moment is a critical one from several of the points of view we have been discussing. This interruption of the narrative is, therefore, more than a characteristic of our poet's style; it is as well more than a feature of the poem's structure; it is in many ways a reflection of the essential problem of the poem. That problem is the poet's presentation of the dual nature of the protagonist — hero and victim — without allowing the hero to become the antithesis of the villain. The latter is quite plainly Satan and we have already observed the demon's flaw: by envying a man he sets up a false dichotomy. The devil is the embodiment of evil, but man cannot be portrayed as evil's antithesis, which would be tantamount to equating man with God. That Garín is the evil demon's victim has been clearly established. The monk's transgression, though brought about as the result of his own volition, finds its origins in the machinations of the devil. In this respect, Garín is the analogue of Adam. In this respect as well, Garín is not Everyman, but simply human. The poet's concern, therefore, is not to allow the protagonist's role as hero to become lost.

Following the symbolic association with Mary Magdalene, Garín and the fleet with which he is traveling continue east along the Mediterranean, heading (again symbolically as well as contextually) for Rome. Within sight of the coast, they are overwhelmed by a sudden storm, Garín being swept overboard and subsequently — miraculously, it would seem — saved. It is at this point that Virués intrudes upon the narrative.

Virués expounds upon "weak human force," thus linking his commentary to the earlier "our mortal weakness" of the initial canto. The allegorical note is thereby sustained. Thereupon, however, the poet steps aside and addresses "man," and employs the second person of the verbs for four consecutive octaves. His subject matter in these strophes is the vanity and haughtiness of man, particularly the futility of mundane aspirations which may embroil miserable man "in the fury of their stirred up sea of misfortunes" because of man's bad conduct which may lead "your shattered boat to the rocks of hell." The metaphor of man's boat amid the angry sea is, of course, one of the oldest of images. Its significance here is more than as an archetypal fulcrum of the poetic narrative. Its use serves to clarify the purposeful nature of the poet's intrusions which remind us of the moralistic intention and the allegorical context. But Virués does not limit this intrusion in canto 7 to a sermon on the vanity of worldly aspirations. Man is contrasted with Garín.

In this new duality, Virués preserves the heroic attributes of his protagonist by contrasting the strength of Garín's penitence with man's pretensions. If "a Garín," who is so repentant is confronted with so many travails, asks the poet, how can man continue to behave in his haughty manner? As I have suggested elsewhere, it is in this context — rather than in bloody scenes of death — that the influence of Seneca emerges in Virués. The stoic philosopher had stressed repeatedly that "the brave stoic soldier will rejoice with each attack of fortune because he realizes that adversity and hardship are the test of his manliness and virtue."[51] The conflict of our poem, therefore, lies not so much between good and evil as it does between virtue and fortune. Here as well we find that "central to the outlook of Seneca is a conception of the eternal struggle between *virtus* and *fortuna*."[52] If it appears that we have repeated ourselves, we should understand a distinction between good and evil on the one hand (moral abstractions), and on the other, fortune and virtue (life's vicissitudes and the individual's behavioral response, respectively). On the moral plane, therefore, Virués sustains the allegory by speaking of man's weaknesses and vices, using Garín's exemplarity as a touchstone against which ordinary humans should test the purity of their aspirations. On the literary level, the poet, conscious of his protagonist's human flaws, emphasizes the monk's unwavering penance and contrition in the face of his enormous sin. Despite that sin, Garín retains an unshakeable faith in God's mercy and a steadfast resolution to see the matter through in the face of the adversities thrown his way. In this manner, Virués preserves the monk's heroic attributes. The author's intrusions are consequently purposeful manipulations of his subject matter. As a result of the poet's interruption in canto 7, we can perceive the significance of the final line of that canto: *everyone* "holds Garín to be a notable man."

IX *Purposeful Digression*

Following universal agreement on Garín's status as a notable man, cantos 8-11 barely mention the monk at all. These four cantos relate in a detailed manner a series of bloody battles between the armada and the Arabs on the African coast of the Mediterranean. A hurried reading might suggest irrelevance, but upon reflection we may perceive purpose once again. Part of that purpose may, of course, reflect the intentional postponing technique of the epic poet, as we noted earlier. But there is more.

The hero of our poem has been confirmed as a notable man, yet we readily observe that the "heroic" qualities are not those of the warrior. To place Garín's moral heroism in relief is the principal function of cantos 8-11, in which a veritable parade of military heroes and heroics is presented to the reader. There is no intent on the part of the poet to belittle the glories of the victories. Our poet is, after all, the same who earlier devoted a panegyric to Lepanto, a digression of another sort which, we have found, provided a complementary ambience for the principal action. In this respect, the lengthier digression in cantos 8-11 serves a similar purpose, as the same polarization of Arab-Christian or infidel-faithful provides the religious background for the Satan-Garín conflict. Although Garín's role in these four cantos appears negligible, a persistent note by the poet reminds us of the monk's presence. Accordingly, amid a description of the Christian forces, Virués will insert a parenthetical reminder that it was these men "with whom Garín may be found," thereby linking the digression to the monk's quest.

Nevertheless, while the digression reinforces the struggle for Christian values, it also serves to set apart the worldly glories of the battlefield from the saintly purpose of Garín. Of several examples we could cite, the most dramatic instance is the role which the monk elects to play with respect to the wounded Arab leader captured by the Christians. Garín asks and is permitted to "be for [the Arab's] body and soul the nurse" (canto 9). The four-canto digression comes to a close with the death of the Arab, while Garín "to his soul gave life with water pure, / then to his body with tears a sepulchre" (canto 11). Garín's role in the conversion of the infidel helps us to perceive the parallels and contrasts of the dualistic portrait of Christian heroism which our poem presents. The "cross and sword" posture finds a dramatic realization in the four cantos under discussion. Seen in this light, the lengthy episode may still be termed a digression, but once again, a purposeful one.

X *The Trials of the Hero*

The distinction between the heroism of our pious protagonist and the heroics of the soldiers is sharpened as the armada reaches Italy and Garín takes leave of his fellow travelers. General Alberto wishes to celebrate the arrival but Garín heads for Rome at once, remaining only long enough to spend the cold night, whereupon "it was not possible to detain him one more hour" (canto 12). Starting out alone for Rome, Garín comes upon a lovely setting amid which is a sumptuous palace and in which he is given lodging. As he falls asleep in the soft bed, Garín's guardian angel once more appears before him and chides him for sleeping in such luxurious surroundings. Warning him that he must remain alert, the angel promises to aid him, always provided that Garín does not stray from the advice given to him. Canto 13 provides the monk with the temptation of the flesh, as a beautiful siren attempts to seduce him. The shape she has assumed is so much like that of the girl he had seduced in Montserrat that Garín has momentary doubts about the latter's being dead. This resemblance not only links this adventure to the beginnings of the poem and reminds us of the purpose of Garín's pilgrimage, but provides us with an indication of Garín's development since the transgression of the earlier cantos. The same beauty no longer leads him astray. Garín "flees victorious" (canto 13).

No sooner has he escaped the temptations of luxury and lust than he finds himself captured by a tribe of cannibals. Garín's attitude in the face of the horrendous death threatening him reflects the dual aspect of the will, analogous to the two kinds of fortune. Similar to providential fortune is the will of God, readily acknowledged to control such paramount matters as life and death, whereas the will of man determines good or evil behavior. Accordingly, Garín prays to God and asks only to be allowed to pass on to heaven, in accordance with God's mercy and Garín's voluntary repentance:

> For thy will is my life or death.
> And so, Lord, with thy will do I in fact
> Place mine into accord most joyful;

The Monserrate

> Only through the mercy of thy bosom
> Only, Lord, only dare I ask
> That through this mortal strait shall pass
> To the wide sea of immortal calm
> My soul, sad now and pained,
> And as it can and ought, repentantly reclaimed.
> (Canto 14)

Garín is rescued by a group of Christian warriors and is at last able to approach Rome. The poet now links the opening canto of the first part of the epic to this closing canto of the second part by relating Satan's fury at Garín's successful pilgrimage:

> Unable was the king of the Tartarean court
> (For of the monk was he a most fierce enemy)
> To stand to see that it was now so short
> A way to good Garín's desired goal to be;
> And heading quick and furious to the north,
> Fierce Aquilo, wind ever unsheltered, summoned he,
> Unleashing from his furious caverns into flight,
> A force which caused the earth to tremble as in fright.
> (Canto 15)

This last in the series of tribulations on the road to Rome is overcome as well and Garín finally gains access to the Vatican. With the granting of an audience with the Pope, Virués closes canto 15 and what we have termed the second part of the *Monserrate*.

XI *Penance*

That one stage has ended and another is about to begin is announced by the poet in several of the concluding strophes of the fifteenth canto. "End of travail it seems to be here, / Start of a greater one now does appear," is a recurrent note in these stanzas, as the poet announces the climactic episodes yet to come. Canto 16 appropriately opens the third and final part of the *Monserrate* with a new appeal to the poetic muse.

The Pope imposes a most extraordinary penance: Garín must crawl on all fours and in this manner return to Montserrat, where he is to remain in this posture until a young babe should tell him otherwise. (In some versions of the legend, Garín imposes this penance upon himself, and only after his return to Montserrat. The version adopted by Virués is consistent with the dual aspect of the will — divine ordination and human compliance — which we have observed throughout the poem.) This ordeal, the very stuff of the genre,[53] is barely described, much less narrated. We are told quite succinctly that the monk passed through Tuscany and Lombardy, across the Alps and the Pyrenees, being returned by his hands and knees to his beloved Montserrat. Seven years later, the narrative continues, Count Jofré, while hunting on Montserrat, comes upon what he takes to be a wild beast, not realizing it is Garín. The latter is taken to Barcelona, where he is kept in captivity until the newborn child of Jofré speaks the words which the Pope had foretold.

In the meantime, in an episode analogous to the birth of Christ, angels have announced to some shepherds of Monistrol (a town at the foot of the mountain) the existence of an image of the Virgin Mary and the Christ Child, thus fusing the legend of the founding of the monastery and the miraculous resuscitation of Garín's victim. The latter is found alive where the monk had buried her and in an "all's well that ends well" atmosphere, the poem ends as Garín prophesies future glories for the Spain of Charles V, Philip II, and Philip III.

XII *A Perspective for the* Monserrate

The plot of the final part of the *Monserrate* is, of course, based on the best-known legends surrounding the famous monastery. Our interest here, accordingly, lies less in the predictable outcome than in Virués's treatment of these climactic cantos. Although our immediate concern in these pages is the poem under discussion, our larger purpose remains Virués's position in the literary development of his culture and time, a position which we have termed pivotal. In this respect, he is perhaps far *more* representative than a Cervantes or a Lope de Vega who, almost by definition, are singular rather than general embodiments of artistic genius. (That Lope as well as Cervantes may readily be described as "typical" or "of the people" is a tribute to these giants' talent for reflecting the aspirations of their people and does not set aside the exceptional nature of their achievements.) In fact, we might even suggest that the repeated praise heaped upon Virués by Lope and Cervantes did not derive its origin exclusively from the merits of the Valencian's works, but was kindled as well by a recognition of similar artistic sensibilities. A Cervantes or a Lope does not portray a people's cir-

The Monserrate

cumstances by rising spontaneously.[54] In this context, then, a Virués may reflect a set of shared artistic inclinations and thereby illustrate what was generally developing (out of which the colossi produced their masterpieces).[55] With the foregoing in mind, we should examine two aspects revealed to us in the final part of the *Monserrate*.

We noted above the rapid manner in which Virués dealt with the penance imposed by the Pope, despite the epic qualities inherent in this heroic struggle to return to Montserrat. The absence of a major episode is particularly remarkable when we recall that the substance of the central part of the poem (cantos 4–15) concerned itself with the voyage from Barcelona to Rome and the obstacles encountered along the way. We can explain this acceleration of events partly by suggesting that the nature of the poem dictated this treatment to the poet. This is not to say that the writer had exhausted his imaginative talent. Rather, in accordance with the underlying religious motif, the thread of the narrative appropriately concerns itself initially with the transgression, then with the struggle to seek absolution in the face of adversity and temptation (the element of suspense), and subsequently the awaiting of the miracle which would release the monk from his penance and convert the mountain (which, symbolically, the devil had sought to dominate) into a holy sanctuary. The distance (in time and space) between Rome and Montserrat following the audience with the Pope has, therefore, no epic significance. Unlike the peregrination toward Rome, the penance of the return to Montserrat contains little pathos from a religious point of view. The Pope's words have made the next important stage the awaiting of the miracle at Montserrat. If the first part of the poem is an analogue of the fall and exile of Adam, then the climactic moment of the final part (redemption of the sinner) finds its analogue in the coming of Christ. As we noted above, the parallel in the manner of the revelation of the Virgin and Child is evident.

It is here, as well, that we find the significance of the anonymity and apparent passivity of the violated girl. It will be recalled that she alone seemed to have no dual aspect in the first part of the poem. The incomplete nature of her character finds its fulfillment in her role as the resurrected personification of divine grace, which "is what you see in me by seeing me alive" (canto 19). The period between the prophecy of the Pope and the miracle at Montserrat is, accordingly, analogous to the "dark ages" prior to the coming of

Christ (prefigured in our poem at the shrine of Mary Magdalene). Although the trials of the hero as he attempted to cross the Alps and the Pyrenees on all fours offered material for pity and suffering, the mind's eye of the reader would naturally leap to the next stage in the religious events, namely, the climax at Montserrat.

More meaningful for an understanding of Virués's art in general, perhaps, is the apparent desire not to elaborate upon a grotesque adventure. Although we are here concerned with epic poetry, specifically a religious epic, we should recall that our poet is generally considered to have been fond of the grotesque, of bloodshed, and of death, in his dramatic endeavors. A generic distinction does not, in itself, clarify matters, for the *Monserrate* contains its share of bloody scenes, ranging from the murder of the seduced girl to the several gory depictions of military encounters. It does not seem farfetched, therefore, to see in the absence of an elaborated succession of horrors — despite the terrors already present in the very nature of the penance — the very plain fact that Virués was not ineluctably drawn to harrowing scenes of awe. Recognizing, as we have suggested, that despite the ready-made horror of the penance, an inordinate emphasis upon this segment of the legend would not serve the purpose of his poem, Virués simply chose not to stress its shocking aspects. Self-evident as this may be, it is of importance for an understanding of Virués's art, for it modifies the observations of so many critics to see in Virués a penchant for horror derived from a Senecan influence. That horror and scenes of bloody death are not uncommon in Virués's works — dramatic as well as epic literature — may indeed be traced to Seneca, but far more significant is the purpose of such scenes and it is Seneca's philosophical (more than literary) position — the response to adversity — that is at the heart of Virués's attitude. We shall see this once more when we comment upon Virués's dramatic works; we emphasize it now as an indication of how Virués's artistic treatment of a Senecan philosophical point of view transcends literary genres. Conversely, by perceiving Virués's ethical understanding irrespective of genre, we may apprehend with less distortion the poet's application of this philosophy in his literature.

In a parallel manner, another glance at Virués's understanding of providence will provide us with a better capability of treating his literary works. We have referred several times to the dual aspect of fortune, namely, divine providence and the vicissitudes of worldly life. That Virués understood this not only in the general way that

The Monserrate

any perceptive human being of his age would have sensed it, but in a very specific way of comprehending the particular distinction, is made clear in some illuminating verses of canto 17:

> Secrets these are of the high Providence
> That by its power sustains the world and rules it,
> To which can reach no earthly human science
> Though it research the heavens and the pit:
> Not star nor fate 'tis nor contingence
> Nor force of the second disposition is it
> Which governs the spherical machine so round,
> But by divine eternal Providence is bound.

The key words for our purpose lie in the sixth line quoted, for by contrasting the "second disposition" — literally, the "second disposing" (*disponer segundo* in the original Spanish) — with the "high Providence," a contrast which is emphasized once more in a subsequent strophe by a reference to the "divine disposition" (*disponer divino*), Virués articulates the dualism to which we have referred so frequently. The point of these strophes is, of course, to stress the primacy of divine providence. Contained within these verses, however, is a recognition of a *second* level, that which is clearly inferior but unquestionably a force in the affairs of "the spherical machine." The unequivocal recognition that man is endowed with a power to dispose — albeit clearly secondary in potency and influence — is, as we have observed, a prominent motif of the *Monserrate*. As we shall now observe, its function is of no small importance for an understanding of Virués's dramatic works as well.

CHAPTER 3

The Response to Fate and Fortune

THE preceding chapter concluded with a reiteration of Virués's understanding of the distinction between the two varieties of fortune or, as we have come to describe them, a divine providence (frequently associated with the will of God) and a mutable fortune (readily identified as the ordinary vicissitudes of life). Although we found it helpful to call upon the observations of scholars on these matters, the narrative framework of the *Monserrate* permitted us to consider the concepts as Virués himself perceived and described them. In the present chapter, as we turn to the works which Virués wrote for the stage, it will be necessary to deduce these matters from the words and actions of the characters, for although the language and the plot are creations of the poet, he is not there to intrude and clarify. As we shall have occasion to discuss in a subsequent chapter, the author's presence does make itself felt in the prologues and epilogues. For the present, however, we must limit our interpretations to the plays themselves.

Earlier we cited Mandel and it is appropriate to do so once more, for the warning he sounds is pertinent to the concerns of the current chapter: "The fatality which reaches us 'out of the blue' is one thing; that which we call upon ourselves by our will and our deed is quite another; and the distinction is so decisive that ... the same term cannot properly be applied to them. Yet though the difference is radical, some critics continue to confuse the two.... [The] theme of uncontrollable fatality is probably older, because more elementary, than that of tragedy. It is illustrated by a whole period, the medieval, in which it was thought to be the very essence of tragedy."[1] It is essential — critically so — to bear in mind the distinction between the two kinds of fortune, as well as to recall that Virués himself saw fit to define that distinction. Accordingly, we know not only that he was aware of the difference but, significantly, that he felt a need to make the distinction explicit, as he did in canto 17 of the *Monserrate.*

We are, of course, dealing with two different literary genres, but the generic distinction need not lead us to assume a corresponding divergence in the author's ethical views. Accordingly, what we have been able to perceive in the *Monserrate,* precisely because its generic framework does not preclude an intrusive author, should be of some aid in our reading of the dramas. Aside from our appreciation of the poem in its own right, we should be able to carry over to the dramas our understanding of Virués's world-view. We need not be surprised to find that this is not an original posture, for works concerning the wiles of the devil, the very existence of which inspire the response of the human will as the dynamic source of conflict, abounded. In a literary vein such works reflected the theological doctrine of free will, as we noted earlier. What is important for us here, therefore, is not to discuss Virués's originality in these matters, for he is quite orthodox — which, in a sense, must necessarily mean conventional — in his understanding and presentation of man's free will. What does assume importance for us is to discern and comprehend what may be taken as conventional philosophical and ethical considerations, when these inform Virués's other works as well. Accordingly, Virués's emphasis on the distinction between divine providence and worldly fortune, with its concomitant implications concerning human responses, must be kept in mind when these matters appear in his dramatic works.

I Elisa Dido

Mindful of the disparate opinions held by scholars with respect to the chronology of *Elisa Dido,* as we pointed out in chapter 1, we may nonetheless deal with this play first, inasmuch as it, more than any other by Virués, reflects the influence of earlier, Classical models. This is not sufficient reason to accept a judgment that *Dido* is Virués's earliest play. Froldi's argument that its extraordinary format may in itself suggest an isolated instance and thus belong to any period of Virués's literary activity, remains a valid hypothesis. Froldi's further postulation that Virués himself felt the need to point out the Classical nature of *Dido* as something exceptional, "an undertaking foreign to his habitual interests,"[2] is an observation rich in its suggestion that Virués was more at ease with an orientation of another sort. We shall return to this point frequently, particularly in the chapter on *Marcela*. For the present, we begin with *Dido* not for reasons of chronology with respect to its composition, but, as indicated, because of its more evident attempt to adhere to Classical modes.

The plot of *Elisa Dido* is as follows: Dido, queen of Carthage, agrees to the demand of Iarbas, king of Mauritania, to marry him, the alternative being an attack upon Carthage. Dido, still in love with her dead husband, Siqueo, must deal as well with her own general, Carquedonio, and her governor, Seleuco, each of whom is opposed to Dido's decision, primarily because each is in love with her. The first act concludes with the invocation of providence by the chorus. The second act is largely concerned with a secondary action: Ismeria, Dido's chambermaid, believes that Seleuco is in love with her, while Delbora, a slave, similarly believes that she is the object of Carquedonio's love. The two men confess their love for Dido, and the act ends with a lament on the tyranny of love, recited by the chorus. In the third act, Iarbas's ambassador delivers gifts for Dido: a crown, a scepter, and a sword. Dido confides to Ismeria her continuing fidelity to the dead Siqueo, but leaves unclarified how she plans to deal with the dilemma. Dido is informed of an attack by the soldiers of Carquedonio and Seleuco upon Iarbas's army. The chorus sings of the bitterness of jealousy as an outgrowth of love. In the fourth act Dido is told of the deaths of Carquedonio and Seleuco in the battle against Iarbas's forces. The chorus laments the power of love over poor soldiers. In the fifth and final act, Iarbas arrives at Dido's chapel, the doors of which are then opened to reveal Dido's dead body, with Iarbas's sword piercing her breast, and his crown and scepter on the floor. A letter written by Dido explains that this was her way to save her people and simultaneously preserve her vow of chastity. Iarbas promises freedom to Carthage and declares Dido to be "goddess of Carthage, [regarded] eternally with sacred worship, honor, and reverence" (p. 177).[3]

Given Virués's own statement that this play adheres to Classical principles, we should not be surprised to find in *Elisa Dido* a strong and repeated emphasis on the power of fate. In the very first scene of the drama, Dido herself refers to it in terms that we recognize from our earlier discussion:

> Fate, which is a divine disposer
> that, by secret ways not understood

> by human knowledge, brief and obscure,
> leads men to certain ends
> for which they were placed in the world
> by the great maker of world and men,
> ....
> as you know, brought me to this land,
> where through self-interest and ingenuity
> I got the needed wherewithal I sought
> to found this city.... (pp. 146–47)

The opening reference to fate as a "divine disposer" (*disponer divino*) is an important clue, for it not only defines but distinguishes the variety of fortune with which we are dealing. It is the divine providence which placed men in the world for reasons known only to the deity. Our reading of the *Monserrate* has prepared us, however, to distinguish divine design from quotidian vicissitudes. As we work our way through the complexities of Dido's sentence — the original is an uninterrupted sentence of eighteen hendecasyllabic lines of blank verse — we observe that the first six lines depict fate's general attributes. By the time we reach the particular matters involving Dido — the grammatical subject of "brought me to this land" is the "fate" of the initial line — we cannot escape observing a significant transition. Fate (or providence) does indeed work in ways incomprehensible to mortals, whom it places in the world and whom it leads to certain ends, as it has led Dido to Carthage. Thereupon, however, Dido speaks of how she herself managed to found the city, as a result of self-interest and ingenuity (*por interesse i por industria*). It seems clear that Dido's drama will be that of responding to fate rather than remaining its plaything.

The point raised here is not limited to a philosophical consideration of fate, fortune, and free will. To a large extent, we are here dealing with the essence of drama. (We should not overlook the etymology: the word itself derives from the Greek *dra,* "to do." Drama, accordingly, deals with what people do.) Although the element of suspense, so fundamental to the theater, inevitably hinges upon developments in the plot, the essence of drama generally tends to center upon the *manner* in which these developments reach their climax.[4] This apparent tautology assumes significance when we recognize how few of even the world's greatest plays depend for their success upon what the outcome is as much as upon how that outcome is reached. Were this self-evident phenomenon not so, audiences would not continue to flock to performances whose endings are known beforehand. For this same reason, originality of plot is rarely synonymous with the ingenious *handling* of familiar material. The spectator is intrigued by the vicarious experience of going through the vicissitudes which confront the characters and of sharing the emotional and intellectual response of the latter. Aristotle, for example, could not have spoken of pity and suffering, much less of catharsis, had he not understood the evident prior requirement of experiencing the complications of the intrigue, as opposed to finding the play's value exclusively, or even principally, in the final moments of purgation. Similarly, in Virués's *Dido,* the essence of this drama lies not so much in the final outcome as in the process, which is to say the drama itself.

In this respect, Sargent's usual perspicacity failed her when she ventured that "Virués needlessly sacrifices any struggle Dido may have experienced when faced by the threatened destruction of her people if she kept her vow to Siqueo, by opening the play with the resultant decision."[5] However, the opening of the play provides us only with her decision to accept Iarbas's matrimonial demands. That decision, as we have noted in our summary, is ultimately converted into a sacrificial self-immolation, quite unlike anything revealed at the beginning of the drama. In fact, it is only in act III that, as Sargent herself summarizes, Dido "declares to Ismeria unswerving fidelity to her dead husband Siqueo, and hints at a secret which she cannot yet share with her."[6] Stated in another way consistent with our observations above, the first-act exposition presents the dilemma: Dido wishes to remain faithful to her dead husband; at the same time, she wishes to preserve peace and the freedom of her people; yet she has agreed to Iarbas's demands, a decision which is opposed by her general and her governor. Although she herself has depicted a grand design under fate's control, she has as well portrayed herself as possessing sufficient ingenuity to act (within the limits imposed by providence). How she will use that ingenuity, how she will act, how she will respond to worldly fortune — these comprise the drama of this play. That she is indeed determined to act is emphasized by her majestic response to Carquedonio and Seleuco when they voice their disapproval of her decision to agree to marry Iarbas: "No matter what new accidents may happen / I do not cease to be the same Elisa; / Elisa Dido am I" (pp. 148-49).[7]

The Response to Fate and Fortune

The verses which the chorus sing to divine providence at the close of the first act do reveal a pagan subordination to a preordained circumstance, but it is difficult to miss the Christian note: along with the deceptions and miseries of this life, there is an inherent quality of mercy in the conception of providence:

> Divine providence,
> ....
> don't abandon the loving
> and sweet companion
> who always accompanies you equally;
> that generous pity
> from whom sad man hopes
> [to receive] his help and consolation,
> let with you always be
> that which in such serious hurts provides for us.
> ....
> for if heaven has no pity for man,
> man is without help and consolation.   (pp. 152-53)

In addition to the Christian quality of mercy — in itself of significance, for it reveals that even in this work Virués was doing something other than an imitation of the Classics — there is implicit in the above some measure of effect *upon* providence. Qualities such as generosity, pity, help, and consolation have little meaning in the abstract, for their effect is realized only in a context of need, which is to say that man may appeal for aid. In short, man may act.

It is interesting to note that from among the dozens of works analyzed in his massive study, Hermenegildo selects *Elisa Dido* as "one work ... in which we find the concepts of fate and providence mixed."[8] To substantiate this observation, Hermenegildo cites two passages from the first act. One is the recitation by the chorus at the conclusion of the act, which we have just cited; the other is Dido's remarks about fate at the beginning, which we cited earlier. Hermenegildo makes a highly perceptive comment about Dido: "The virile energy of the heroine and the deep affection that she feels for the memory of Siqueo, produce in her the certainty that destiny is a most important part of the struggle of imponderables which her existence has set in motion."[9] What Hermenegildo has perceived is not only the point he is establishing, namely, the "desire to fuse destiny and providence [which] Virués reveals in the work cited."[10] In Hermenegildo's words we recognize a heroine of virile energy whose existence is caught up in a struggle of imponderables. Herein lies the essence of the drama to which we have been alluding: the outcome is secondary to the struggle, and inherent in the terms "struggle" and "virile energy" is the potentiality of dealing with the "imponderables." In one sense, we may view the outcome as classically tragic: the heroine dies and we may take as an indication of her moral flaw her prevarication with respect to her agreement to marry Iarbas. Yet, such an interpretation does not ring true. In fact, as one of Dido's captains points out, by (apparently) acquiescing to Iarbas's demands, Dido "is damning herself by giving herself to a barbarian; and we similarly are being damned" (p. 153). At the same time, Dido maintains that her goal is "for peace, for holy peace" (p. 147). Therein lies her dilemma and the conflict of the drama: to avoid damnation and achieve holy peace. Her prevarication, therefore, is intended to resolve this conflict. As Crawford has observed, "Her reply is a diplomatic lie, and the interest is concentrated upon this fallacious answer and her suicide in the presence of her suitor."[11]

McKendrick is correct when she refers to Dido's "qualities of courage and resolution, prudence and shrewdness,"[12] although it seems somewhat exaggerated to consider her "a superwoman on a heroic scale."[13] In any event, most observers seem to be in agreement with respect to Dido's virile qualities and the fact that her struggle is the central aspect of the drama.[14] That struggle may *appear* to be against fate or providence, in which case her death would be considered the tragic end, the fall of the heroic queen, as we suggested (and rejected) above. Yet providence is guiding her, not opposing her, and therein lies the significance of the chorus's recognition of mercy as a concomitant of providence. All of Dido's aims — the preservation of her chastity, the salvation of her people, holy peace — are in accord with the will of providence.

Throughout the play we are given to understand that Dido is in heaven's favor.[15] Her thoughts and behavior follow the advice of her dead husband, who had received special dispensation to return to her after his death (p. 150), whereupon Dido promised to obey the "order which on heaven's behalf you brought me" (p. 158), specifically explained later as Dido's having promised to Siqueo chastity ever since that moment (p. 176). As the drama progresses, we are informed that Dido's "spirit is divine" (p. 168), along with Delbora's prophetic wish that "heaven allow her to prosper, and provide her with glorious death and eternal, illustrious fame" (p. 169). This has prepared us for the representation of Dido as a goddess after her death. Virués has taken advantage of the pagan elements to reinforce the divine level of fortune, i.e., providence, which provides guidance — often in unfathomable ways — and which the virtuous queen obeyed.

But the drama presents a thoroughly human struggle, revolving around the machinations of mortal beings and their temporal conflicts. What Crawford has described as Dido's diplomatic lie is indicative of the two planes. On the grand scale and in consonance with the designs of providence, Dido is not guilty of dishonesty, for she maintains her virtue by preserving her chastity, symbolic of her respect for the eternal verities. In contrast, the vicissitudes of this life presented by worldly fortune require a different sort of response. On this level Dido is anything but fortune's toy and the drama of her responses to the challenges in her life — the threat to the freedom of her people, the prospect of a marriage not based on mutual love,[16] the attitudes of her subordinates — is what arouses our interest as spectators. Accordingly, in *Elisa Dido* we find both levels of fortune operative in the development of the play. The grand design is that of providence, but the jealousies, ambitions, desires, and machinations of mortals become the ups and downs of those whom they affect. On this level, the fortunes and misfortunes confronting human fortitude require a response of the will. Dido's resolution triumphs over these obstacles, and so her death is readily viewed as heroic. It is not her downfall, but "the great victory which I achieve with my death" (p. 176).

II Great Semíramis

Although we are unable to place *Elisa Dido* in a chronological sequence in the composition of Virués's plays, much less attribute it to a specific year, we should naturally expect to find some meaningful contrasts between *Dido,* written "in accordance with the old style" (prologue, p. 146), and *Semíramis,* a work which Virués tells us was written in the "new style" (prologue, p. 25). Since we do know that *Semíramis* is the first of the remaining four plays,[17] all of which are composed in the so-called new style, it is appropriate to move now to this most frequently published of Virués's dramas.[18]

We may summarize the plot as follows: Nino, king of Assyria, holds the city of Bactra under siege but has not succeeded in subduing it. Semíramis, wife of General Menón, suggests a plan of attack which proves successful, thereby attracting Nino's attention.

The king falls in love with her and expresses his desire to marry her, offering to Menón the hand of his daughter in exchange. Menón refuses, Nino takes Semíramis nonetheless, and Menón hangs himself. Act II takes place sixteen years later. Nino agrees to Semíramis's request to allow her to rule for a period of five days. Semíramis avails herself of Zelabo and Zopiro, two soldier-servants, the former imprisoning Nino and the latter (with whom Semíramis carries on a love affair) instructing Ninias (son of Nino and Semíramis) to confine himself to the temple of the vestal virgins, dressed in his mother's clothes. For her part, Semíramis assumes Ninias's clothes and pretends to be her son. Informing the council that "Semíramis" has retired to the temple and that Nino has been taken to heaven in the form of a dove, Semíramis proceeds to rule disguised as the prince. Brought before what he takes to be Ninias, Nino assumes Semíramis to have been killed and willingly accepts the poison Semíramis had prepared for him. The third and final act takes place six years later. Semíramis, at last dressed as a woman once more, reveals her identity to the council. Ninias, now king, is disgusted to learn that his mother feels sexually attracted by him. Ninias kills his mother, Semíramis's lowly origins and licentious life are revealed, and Ninias describes how Semíramis ascended to heaven converted into a dove.

Even this brief synopsis cannot fail to invite a comparison between *Great Semíramis* and *Elisa Dido,* particularly between the two protagonists. The evident antithetical attitudes to circumstances which display striking parallels merit some attention in a chapter dealing with responses to life's challenges.

McKendrick has observed the complementary nature of the two plays, although we may wish for less hyperbole as she suggests that these two works "may be grouped together in that both have as protagonist a superwoman on a heroic scale. Here the similarity ends, for whereas Queen Dido ... is a paragon of womanly and queenly virtue — the epitome of female *varonilidad* [virility] in its most flattering sense — Semíramis ... is a woman of tragic faults."[19]

The contrasts are indeed striking. Whereas Dido became queen as a consequence of her husband's murder (an event belonging to the play's prehistory and narrated by Ismeria), Semíramis's ascent to the throne is the result of her murder of her husband (although technically Nino's death is an induced suicide, as was the death of Semíramis's first husband). In both plays, a king demands the hand

The Response to Fate and Fortune

of the woman in question: in Dido's case, her fidelity to her dead husband becomes a motivating force in her resistance to Iarbas's importuning; in Semíramis's case, her infidelity to her living husband paves the way for her accession to power. In both situations, the relationship of the woman to the importunate king is tied to a military siege: Dido attempts to prevent bloodshed; Semíramis plots military victory. In both plays, the heroine dies: Dido willingly and Semíramis at the hands of her son. Both deaths are presented to the people as ascents to heaven: the reverence of her people causes Dido's memory to assume a divine aspect; the evident mendacity of Ninias's account of his mother's death negates the parallel attempt to attribute divine status to Semíramis.[20] Finally, it goes without saying that whereas Dido displays virtue, Semíramis embodies vice.

In order to examine the role of fortune and fate in *Great Semíramis* it becomes necessary, in fact inescapable, to deal with the portrayal of tragic figures.[21] Although it is generally accepted that *Elisa Dido* belongs to the tragic mode, our comments made earlier with respect to the nature of Dido's death — portrayed not as a fall but as an ascent to heaven and divine status — permit some equivocation. We may nonetheless agree that in *Dido* Virués dramatizes the rise and fall (from earthly power) of a heroic personage of noble caste. It is this last point which is too often glossed over in analyses of *Semíramis*. Although it appears to be no more than a point, the following relevant excursion will serve to show its importance.

Rigidity with respect to the Classical precepts cannot be said to be characteristic of Spanish authors generally, and this assessment naturally includes Virués as well. Nonetheless, the theoreticians of antiquity continued to serve as authorities, although it must be understood that such authority was disparately interpreted not only by the poets themselves, but by the intermediary sources (primarily Italian) from whom they had received translations of Aristotle and Horace, among many others. Moreover, not only the translations but the commentaries which accompanied them varied considerably. What is of importance to us, of course, is not so much what Aristotle really had in mind as how the theoreticians and poets of the Renaissance interpreted the treatises. The point that bears upon our study is the understanding of character in a tragedy. For a quick reference, the passage in question appears as follows in a modern English version of Aristotle's *Poetics:* "Homer imitated superior men and Hegemon of Thasos, the inventor of parody..., inferior ones.... Finally, the difference between tragedy and comedy coincides exactly with the master difference: namely the one tends to imitate people better, the other one people worse, than the average."[22]

The first Renaissance exposition of the *Poetics* was that of Robortello (1548). Weinberg has translated the relevant portion as follows:

For Aristotle meant ... that the tragic action is not drawn from the fault of just any man who might be of the people and of unknown origin.... Therefore, Aristotle very cleverly posited these two things: first, a grave and great fault, and then that the hero should fall from happiness to misery. For these things cannot happen at the same time to anybody unless he be a man of the highest authority and dignity and placed by fortune in the highest degree of happiness.... It is thus sufficiently clear that common men of low birth cannot sink to calamity from a happiness which they never have possessed.[23]

This explication by Robortello receives the following lucid analysis by Weinberg:

Tragedy will present no wicked persons. Robortello explains what he means by "wicked" in his elucidation of *Poetics* 1448^{a}4, where Aristotle had distinguished between men like ourselves and men better or worse than ourselves. He takes "better" as meaning "superior to those who live in our times...." These are the heroes of epic and gnomic poetry, the kings and heroes of tragedy.... "Worse" means those who are morally base, "those who have the appearance of bad and dishonorable things." But it may also mean those who are of low station in life.... As a matter of fact, as Robortello works with the distinction, it becomes more completely a social than an ethical one.[24]

No one can dispute that Semíramis's character is "wicked," no matter what the particular definition may be. Moreover, she is clearly "morally base." If we are to interpret Aristotle or his Renaissance commentators as referring primarily to moral flaws, it is evident that Semíramis is not qualified for the role of a tragic heroine. The other side of the perennial argument, namely, that the tragic flaw may be interpreted as low social station, and which, as Weinberg has observed, merges with ethical considerations in Robortello's reading, is also present in Virués's play and therein

The Response to Fate and Fortune

lies the importance of the revelation toward the end of the work. As Ninias prepares the fabrication with respect to his mother's supposed end in heaven, Zelabo informs us of her origins: Semíramis was the daughter of a "vile and lowly man" and of a prostitute (p. 54). Given our cursory glance at Aristotelian and neo-Aristotelian definitions of subjects fit for tragic heroism, we can recognize the importance of the revelation of Semíramis's lowly origins. When this information is combined with her moral baseness, one conclusion is unavoidable: we are not dealing with Classical tragedy. It remains possible, of course, to suggest an original conception of tragedy, as A. A. Parker has done for Calderón.[25] However, we assuredly ought not to force Virués's drama into a neo-Aristotelian mold, as McKendrick does when she maintains that "Semíramis is the victim of Fate — her tragedy is that she was not born a man."[26] Far more perceptive is Sargent's comment: "No finer inclinations mark the moral fall of the criminal a dramatic reality; consequently [the criminal's] ultimate worldly fall fails to inspire the terror Virués obviously intended."[27] With respect to Semíramis, Sargent makes a discerning observation, although it is limited to the comparison of incest in the Phaedra and Oedipus of the Classical theater with that of Virués's protagonist. Sargent notes that "whereas Phaedra shudders at the precipice into which her ill-fated love is pushing her against her better instincts, and Oedipus adjusts his whole life to avoid the disaster for which the Fates destine him, Semíramis approaches the crime with the relish of an already perverted degenerate."[28]

Sargent does not follow through on her insightful use of the word "already," a perception which we should link to the revelation of Semíramis's base origins. Accordingly, the protagonist is not endowed with the qualities of the tragic hero (as the neo-Aristotelians would define the term), despite McKendrick's persistence in seeing "much of the tragic hero in Semíramis. Her faults are pride, ambition and latent promiscuity..., and Fate in the person of the king's general intervenes and places her in a position where these faults can flourish."[29] This brings us back to the principal concern of the present chapter. The apparent compulsion to see tragedy and its concomitant motif of fate as the dominant force is, I submit, an inappropriate way to comprehend the characters and their behavior.[30]

The very opening of the play indicates an act of volition with respect to personal identity and purpose, attitudes which we cannot accommodate easily to the concept of fate. Semíramis appears on the battlefield dressed as a man. Leaving to one side the many other interpretations that have been and may be made about this guise — none of which contradicts the basic point being made here — it is evident that this is an act of the will. Whether it reflects a virile character, a wily female, a perversity, or a literary stock in trade, her appearance in this place and in this manner reflects volition.

It is scarcely "fate in the person of the king's general [that] intervenes and places her in [this] position," as Semíramis's own words make clear. Her explanation is replete with irony, given what we know of her character and the subsequent events.[31] She tells Menón that if she were to "become universal queen of the world, [this] would be secondary to seeing you" (p. 26). (Nino, whom she will soon marry, and whose crown she will appropriate, is described only moments later as "king of the world" [p. 29]). In the event that the audience did indeed accept her words to Menón at face value, Virués has her subsequent response reveal that her priorities are quite the reverse of those expressed in the lines just quoted. In reply to Menón's declaration of love, Semíramis briefly echoes her husband's sentiments, stressing that he can judge this by her having undertaken this trip in the strange clothes she is wearing. The irony of her implied duplicity should not escape us, but there is nothing veiled in her hurried desire to change the subject and speak instead of military matters:

> But let us leave things so well known
> as are our mutual desires,
> ....
> tell me the things that have occurred
> in the great rebellion of these cities,
> and the point of the war, and some deed
> of your valorous arm and breast. (p. 26)

It is at this point that Menón laments his failure to achieve victory, whereupon Semíramis provides him with a plan that is successful. Grateful, Menón praises her ingenuity, valor, and intelligence, as Nino lauds the prudence and fortitude of those who achieved the victory. That it was a combination of prudence and fortitude is of no small significance.[32] Whether we wish to argue that warfare is the result of human machinations or that it is in fortune's hands, the response to its challenges is what interests us here. (Needless to say, references to the fortunes of war abound.) Accordingly, it seems clear that the response in the siege of Bactra was one of pru-

The Response to Fate and Fortune

dence (in the sense explained in note 32) on the part of Semíramis, and fortitude on the part of the soldiers.

Left alone with Semíramis, Nino is physically aroused by her. There is again much irony in his insistence that she has come from heaven, that she is an angel from paradise, and that she is divine. The use of conventional metaphors from the vocabulary of love poetry is, with respect to the particular choice of image, shrewdly chosen to underscore the fallacy in the comparison: far from being angelic, we know Semíramis to be diabolic. (From our reading of the *Monserrate* we have come to appreciate Virués's revealing use of what may too easily be dismissed as trite poetry.) With respect to the setting, the incongruous amatory verse amid battlefield surroundings directed at a married woman dressed in masculine attire and following upon her display of military prowess, constitutes a further warning that we are not to interpret the dialogue literally. There follows a casuistic aside, in which Nino debates the pros and cons of making love to Semíramis, by force if necessary, ending with his determination to do so, "since fortune has given me / opportunity, time, and place" (p. 30).

Let us accept the fact that it was fortune, for our concern lies not in debating the existence of this element in the drama, but rather in the responses to it. What remains clear, then, is that one cannot attach to fortune the responsibility for the manner in which the two individuals react to their meeting in these circumstances. Nino subsequently blames the power of love, but what is of significance is that his behavior in the face of supernatural forces like fortune and love is not the response of just any man, but that of a sovereign whose "will is law" (p. 31). Similarly, Semíramis anticipates Nino's plans, and although she does mention the impropriety of his desires, she does not speak of sin. Rather, her first thought is of self-domination — "it is a greater thing to conquer oneself / than to conquer all the world" — followed by a consideration of the social inequities involved: "that a king so powerful / ... / should forcibly make himself spouse / of the wife of his servant" (p. 31).[33] The "logic" that Nino employs in response is to insist upon the will of the king as settling the issue of force. In fact, he will be so courteous as to ask Menón: "since I am your king I ask of you / what by power I can readily have" (p. 32). As for the inequality of social status, by marrying him, proclaims Nino, Semíramis will have "status equal to the [willful] spirit that resides in [her]" (p. 31).[34] Finally, with respect to what attracted Nino's interest in Semíramis, he states unequivocally that it was her *industria* on the battlefield (p. 36).

It is in the second act that we become aware not only of Semíramis's obvious evil qualities but of her driving force to assert her will and have things her way. If it was fate that led her from one husband to another; if it was fortune that raised her from a general's wife to a king's queen; then it was her self-assertion in responding to these circumstances that led her to be more of a soldier than her military husband, Menón, and it was this same exertion of will that led her to be monarch in place of her royal husband, Nino. Although she pays brief lip service to thoughts of revenge for her abduction, the action takes place sixteen years after those events and her soliloquy reveals her true frustration: "sixteen years in which [captivity] reigns in me / with a title of queen without being queen" (p. 39). Semíramis carries the matter an important step further. Driving Nino to suicide and driving their son to the temple, she assumes the latter's robes and reigns not as queen but as king. In addition to the various forms of perversion that have been perceived by a number of critics, this new and lengthy (half a dozen years) adventure in male attire allows her literally to dramatize her character as one of volition personified.

There occurs at this point (almost precisely the midpoint of the second act and consequently of the play itself) a sort of monologue on the role of fortune in the events we have been discussing. (I say "sort of monologue" because it is spoken by Zopiro and Zelabo; however, not only is its effect that of a soliloquy but the Zopiro-Zelabo pair presents throughout the play the semblance of single personality.)[35] Because the essence of this segment is central not only to this play but to the concerns of the present chapter, a lengthy translation here is in order:

> Oh, fortune! Is anything equal
> to your wheel in lightness?
> Is there a current to which is not in excess
> the current of yours perennial?
> Yesterday Nino was monarch
> ....
> and today he is a sad captive
> ....
> Consolation is born therefrom
> for me from a hope not strange
> that since in everything there is change,
> there may be as well in me some.
> Am I not the one who was yesterday
> of the king but a poor squire

The Response to Fate and Fortune

>   and today have I not reached higher
>   to be waiting on the queen, his lady?
>   ....
>   What a funny thing it would surely be
>   if I should now succeed Nino!
>   But, how could I imagine a thing so?
>   What lightheaded fantasy that'd be!

Zelabo responds:

>   Let Nino give up the throne and bow
>   to Semíramis, queen for now,
>   and if things for us better now unfold,
>   a hundred thousand years let her it hold.
>   .... (pp. 41-42)

The passage includes several references to the familiar metaphor of the wheel of fortune and related conventional remarks about fortune's mutability. Hermenegildo cites the first quatrain of the above and observes: "Lack of confidence in fortune is one of the truths that Virués attempts to inculcate in his public on many occasions."[36] There can be no quarrel with the observation as a general remark; one might almost say that the remark applies to most literature of the age, always provided that we are speaking of worldly fortune and not divine providence. Curiously, in the passage under discussion the statement does not find its typical exposition unless we were to limit our perusal to the initial four lines quoted by Hermenegildo. The ultimate moral may indeed be as Hermenegildo succinctly puts it, but the passage in question, which begins by expressing renewed wonder at the ups and downs of fortune, progressively asserts the benefits of seizing upon these moments of opportunity. Morals and moralizing aside — into these we have some insight from our reading of the *Monserrate* — the *dramatic* possibilities lie in the response to the contingencies of life.[37] Ludicrous as it may be — Zopiro himself says it would be "funny" — yesterday's valet is today's confidant and lover of the queen, ruminating on the possibility of becoming the next king. The political, social, and ethical interpretations we might wish to make of this are undoubtedly obvious as well as risible. For the matter at hand, however, the analysis is equally evident yet not at all ridiculous, for it subsumes the motivations of all the characters in the drama. There is no lament with respect to fortune's unpredictable ways; rather there is a *carpe diem* reaction.

The foregoing is so essential to our appreciation of the drama that we must be cautious not to confuse ethical considerations with dramatic opportunities. "Morals and moralizing aside," we have said, and this is not to imply that such considerations are in fact to be relegated to the periphery. The ultimate "moral" of the plays is indeed an ethical stance, whether we analyze the obvious (vice is vicious; sin is sinful; lust for power is a powerful lust) or the allusive (e.g., Hermenegildo's cited thesis that the courtly intrigue and adulation find their analogue in the corruption of the court of Philip II). However, while we cannot deny an ultimate moralizing purpose, it is equally clear that Virués understood that the *dramatic* benefits lay more in the iniquitous than in the innocuous, just as the interests of a theatrical audience lay more in the immoral than in the immortal.[38] That Virués realized this is apparent not only from an examination of the plays themselves but from his own words about the dramas, as we shall have occasion to observe in our chapter on his prologues.

With the foregoing in mind, particularly the caution which is implicit in our note 37, we need to examine with special care the final two quatrains pronounced by Zopiro in this central passage of the play:

> Well do I see that while we're alive
> thus through extremes along
> we pass from the day we're born
> till at our death we arrive,
> which, if it is good, 'tis of no import
> whether to the rapid wheel we're bound,
> as life goes round and round,
> for a spin that's long or short.   (p. 42).

It is all too easy to dismiss these lines for the trite conventionalism that they comprise. The message defies exegesis by its very simplicity: life is a series of rapid ups and downs but a "good" death makes the spinning wheel of worldly fortune irrelevant. We could as well expound on the implications of a good death and find ourselves entangled in another philosophical and literary commonplace, namely the art of dying, particularly of dying well. But we must not let ourselves be led astray into a maze of philosophizing in the very middle of a play, especially when we do not lose sight —

and the play's audience assuredly did not — of the nature of the speaker. Here is no chorus, no allegorical figure, no noble hero reviewing his tragic errors. The speaker is a lackey whose very existence is guided by the temporal turns of fortune's wheel. Only moments earlier did we hear him speculate about the possibility of rising as high as the throne itself. As for his subsequent behavior, Zopiro becomes one of Semíramis's many lovers.

If we are to see didacticism here, it lies of course in the presentation of behavior *not* to be followed. What is of significance for the present chapter, however, is that Zopiro is exemplary in quite another sense: he typifies lip service to eternal values and concerns about divine responses while leading a life that is determined by worldly considerations. The characters in this play seize upon what they have been taught to perceive as the mutability of fortune. Their sole concern is to benefit, however briefly, from the contingencies which are presented to them. Menón benefits from the masculine qualities of his wife, brings the siege to a victorious conclusion and in the process loses his wife to his king as a result of those very masculine attributes which moments earlier had brought glory. Nino, attracted by Semíramis's talents for command, loses the command of his throne as a result of those very talents. Ninias, the weakest of the lot, is repulsed by his mother's incestuous advances but can combat perversity only with murder. The irony that is contained in all of this is not only that those who ostensibly see through the fallacy of fortune's power nonetheless await its ascending turns in order to rise with it, but rather that it has not been fortune's wheel but Semíramis's will that has set the events in motion. Not luck but Semíramis's machinations lead Menón, Nino, Ninias, and Semíramis herself up the ladder of success and over the brink of failure. So, too, the insignificant Zopiro rises with Semíramis and, victim of her devilry (not fortune's whims), he dies in her bed of lechery (p. 54). *Great Semíramis* may well be called a study of evil personified in a variety of self-serving characters; what it assuredly cannot be called is a play about helpless victims of fortune.

III   Cruel Cassandra

To summarize the plot of *La cruel Casandra* (Cruel Cassandra) is no easy task. Mérimée long ago complained that in this play "complexity and obscurity go hand in hand. It would require many pages to analyze this entangled intrigue, where the unforeseen, from beginning to end, competes with incoherence."[39] Sargent also refers to the "intricate plot,"[40] and Hermenegildo echoes Mérimée: "The first thing we must point out is the extraordinary complexity of the plot.... It is the most complicated of the five tragedies of Virués."[41] With this in mind, let us attempt to summarize the work as follows:

The prince and his servant, Filadelfo, ruminate on the significance of the state of depression in which they had noticed Fulgencia, the prince's lover. Cassandra interrupts to tell the prince that her brother Fabio needs protection because he had defended Filadelfo's character in response to Fulgencia's accusation that Filadelfo is the lover of the princess (i.e., the prince's wife). For her part, Fulgencia tells the prince that she has been seduced by Fabio, allegedly in order to avenge himself upon the prince for the latter's having dishonored Cassandra. We subsequently learn that Cassandra and Fabio are determined to make life difficult for the other principals in the play. This unity is short-lived in view of Cassandra's interest in a lover, Leandro, despite Fabio's objections. Accordingly, the latter enlists the aid of his younger brother Tancredo in a campaign to break up the Cassandra-Leandro relationship. In the second act, Filadelfo receives a letter from Cassandra (with whom he is in love), asking him to meet her in the princess's chambers. The prince is directed to the same place so that he may catch Filadelfo there. In the last act, we learn that the prince has killed Filadelfo, and that in a duel between Tancredo and Leandro, the two men have killed each other. Cassandra seeks vengeance; the prince, having killed the princess, now comes upon Fabio and Fulgencia in a compromising situation, whereupon he kills Fabio and in the exchange of sword strokes is himself killed, while both Fulgencia and Cassandra are recipients of mortal wounds in the skirmish. The king appears and voices his dismay as the play ends.

In an earlier study I remarked that I find *Cruel Cassandra* "the least satisfying of all of Virués's dramas" and that I agreed with Atkinson that every one of the deaths in this play is void of inner necessity, as well as that "no amount of searching will find virtue succoured in the course of *La cruel Casandra*."[42] This evaluation remains valid insofar as it describes dramatic literature, most especially if we are seeking adherence to ethical and psychological presentation of character in the tragic tradition. Nothing we may wish to say, no matter what our perspective, can make of *Cruel Cassandra* anything approaching great theater. Yet, if we cannot perceive great dramatic literature in this play, this is not to say that we can discern no intentions in the work worthy of serious comment.

"The reader is confused not so much because of [this play's] intricacies, as by its obscurities."[43] This is an insightful remark, for it suggests that we turn away from ridicule of the plot's complex entanglements and consider the work not for its artistic merits — which we have already judged to be minimal — but for what it may reveal about Virués's intentions.[44] Sargent evidently finds some of the obscurities intriguing, for she expresses a wish for "a philosophical soliloquy on the part of a disinterested spectator."[45] An extremely interesting conjecture about the obscurities is Hermenegildo's suggestion — which is in accord with his general view concerning Virués's attitude toward court corruption — that perhaps *Cassandra* does not reflect Virués's inexpertness as much as it is "the result of the intention of the author who tried to present to us the monstrous absurdity of a court in which the circumstances are understood only with difficulty."[46] Earlier, Hermenegildo had suggested that in this play "Virués did not cast aside the classical tragic element but tried to place it in reach of an audience with a modern mentality."[47] If Hermenegildo's intuition is carried to its intriguing next step, we would find ourselves with a poet whose works reflect the anticipation of the theater of the absurd. The anachronism may not be as gratuitous as a first reading might imply.[48]

Sargent suggests that in *Cassandra* "one glimpses also a less familiar line of thought. One wonders if Virués is approaching, back in the sixteenth century, the rising peril of the feministic [sic] movement. For Cassandra was obviously a rebel to the existing order for feminine society...."[49] McKendrick agrees that Cassandra "is a rebel against masculine authority and against the social convention that she is subject to this authority even in that matter which concerns herself most closely — marriage."[50] She then adds: "Nearer the truth, perhaps, is the possibility that Virués was unconcerned by the feminist or social implications of this part of the plot."[51]

For a play that is generally judged to be a failure the above indicates a good deal of interest. Most of that interest centers on the protagonist, a "woman who is an artist in crime."[52] That words like "artist" and "rebel" are so commonly applied to Cassandra reflects our interest in her in this chapter. If we do not have disinterested characters providing philosophical observations on the ethical significance of the drama, we do not lack Cassandra's own statement of her "philosophy" in a brief soliliquy:

> The daring are favored by Fortune;
> this I dare to do and already I see
> it placed almost in the halo of the moon.[53]
> I say that without a doubt I believe,
> in view of the progress of this event
> that with my desire fulfilled I shall leave
> and it will be obvious and patent   (p. 87).

Herein lies our interest in the character: the verses present one further example of a conventional metaphor (the wheel of fortune) employed not in the service of the goddess of luck but in a context of the individual's self-confidence. It is, of course, true that Cassandra speaks of being "favored by Fortune," but it is not necessary to resort to exegesis to see that one must be bold and daring in order to warrant such favor. As in similar cases we have discussed, we must distinguish between the "moral" of the story and the drama of the situation. If the "point" of the play is indeed to portray the vice and corruption of the court — and there is no reason to differ with such a view — then it becomes necessary to focus upon the ending. All the principal characters having been killed, the king makes one of his rare appearances in this play in order to conclude the work by voicing his dismay at the catastrophic events. "The king is introduced apparently for the sole purpose of serving as lone surviver [sic] to express mystification at the multiple murders," observes Sargent.[54] Of course, if we consider court corruption as the theme, the minor role played by the king finds its explanation as well in decorum, in the emphasis on the courtiers as the practitioners of corruption, and in the ignorance of these machinations on the part of the monarch.

It is this last point in particular that relates to our immediate concerns. The king in this play, unlike the Attila of the next work to be discussed, does not represent overt iniquity. His concern has been for peace and happiness, but that sentiment has not been translated into regal dominance: either through his weakness or through his myopia, the evils of courtly life among those of influence have been permitted to flourish. Stated another way, while lords and ladies sought to be "daring" and courted not the king's but fortune's favor the monarch allowed chaos to reign. The relationship of chaos (harmony turned disorder) to fortune (happenstance in lieu of hierarchy) is clear: a surrender to haphazard circumstance rather than an authoritative hegemony is tantamount to abdication to fortune's whims and produces chaos. By remaining oblivious to fortune's ups and downs, the king allowed others to provide the realm's responses. These others were sufficiently daring to produce the catastrophic results of our play. The contrast between their selfish and chaotic behavior on the one hand, and the king's passive role on the other, reflects the topsy-turvy ambience of this play. The substance of the king's lament is a twofold confession of his ignorance. Not only does he express his bewilderment in the face of the nefarious events; he voices as well his failure to understand how this state of affairs could exist without his knowledge. The political ineptitude and its resultant moral depravity that the king's concluding monologue confirms support Hermenegildo's oft-cited thesis. What relates that view to the matters dealt with here is the response to fortune: the king has no response; the courtiers — most notably Cassandra herself — eagerly prepare themselves to seize the wheel of fortune on its upward journey. The moral is not that the wheel must also continue for its inevitable descent; rather, that fortune's opportunities left to self-serving courtiers instead of the sober response of a scrupulous morality will lead to chaos and the fall of sovereign and subject alike.

IV Furious Attila

In the play just discussed we came upon an anonymous king whose fault was disregard for the iniquitous behavior of his court. Now we find in *Atila furioso* (Furious Attila) a king whose name in legend and history is recognized as the very personification of iniquity, the scourge of God.[55]

The king, Attila, is enjoying an affair with Flaminia, having installed her in the palace under the nose of the queen by having "Flaminio" disguised as a page. In this masculine attire "Flaminio" has aroused the passion of the queen. Gerardo, a courtier, is in love with the queen, a relationship encouraged by Flaminia. In the manner of Semíramis and Cassandra, Flaminia seeks power through her machinations. In the second act, she agrees to a rendezvous with the queen but sends Gerardo to the nocturnal meeting in her stead, having first made certain that Attila will witness the scene. The result is the "honor killing" of the adulterous queen at the hands of her offended husband, Attila. Other events bring to Attila's attention the captive queen of Dalmatia, Celia, whose beauty arouses Attila's passion, forcing Flaminia to occupy once more a less prominent role than she had hoped to play and, as we might expect, causing her to seek vengeance. In the third act we are informed that Attila, having consumed a poison prepared by Flaminia, lost his senses and has killed Celia. Subsequently, thinking that Flaminia is Death personified, he wrestles with her, kills her, and falls dead as the poison takes its final toll.

Although this play offers much food for thought, its concerns with fortune are limited and references to this concept extremely few. This in itself is of interest, for in those few instances in which fortune is discussed, only one side is presented: the negative. In the other plays we have dealt with so far, the concept of fortune had been portrayed either as mutability in general — that is, the ups and downs — or with a stronger emphasis on the opportunities (the ups) to which humans may respond while aware of the eventual counteraction (the downs). In *Attila,* the characters ascribe to fortune only events of an adverse nature. This may be confined to brief moments of frustration, as is the case of the king of Slovenia, who attributes his defeat at the hands of Attila's forces to "those barbaric flags / which unjust fate so strongly favors" (p. 102). Attila himself blames his downfall on "the rapid wheel of fortune, / torment of miserable mortals" (p. 115). That his death is the result of Flaminia's poison, which in turn is the consequence of Flaminia's ambition and concurrent frustration, in turn kindled by Attila's lust for Flaminia and disregard for his marriage, only serves to reinforce the unconvincing nature of any argument which would have us see fortune as a decisive influence.

The longest passage on fortune is spoken by Flaminia in the second act, after she has overheard the king promise Celia the queen's place on the throne. Furious, Flaminia expresses her frustration:

> Oh, fortune. In a single moment
> you make a hundred thousand movements;
> barely do you provide contentment
> when a hundred thousand discontents
> in its wake are sent.
> Oh, what an enemy of mine
> you show yourself, fortune capricious,

> for when I most did pine,
> you take from me with hand malicious
> the one good thing I had as mine!   (p. 106)

This passage is of significance for us for a number of reasons. We have already noted that in this play references to fortune are primarily concerned with the descent of fortune's wheel (although once more one cannot escape the corresponding ascent implicit in the metaphor). This emphasis on fortune as the source of misfortune, particularly on the part of such strong-willed characters as Attila and Flaminia, places in relief that they believe their successful ventures to have been the result of their own efforts. The traditional metaphor of fortune's wheel — especially the wheel's rapidity of rotation — reflects the theme of mutability and its suddenness, but unlike the passages in the other plays dealt with in this chapter, explicit reference to a rise in one's fortune by the characters of *Attila* does not attribute a better change to a better chance.

In the same passage just quoted, following Flaminia's having associated the frustration of her carefully laid plans with fortune's fickleness, she abruptly shifts the blame:

> My parents, relatives, and siblings
> in a war unjust and inhumane
> you took from me, you tyrant king,
> and brought me here to your terrain
> in this attire most unbecoming;
> and because of you I did believe
> that 'twas I whom you adored,
> forgot the insult I did receive,
> and as my friend and lord
> to you with love and fealty did cleave.   (*ibid.*)

From a lament on the inconstancy of fortune Flaminia has turned to an acknowledgment of the inconstancy of Attila. If this is not a complete shift from a superhuman force to human volition, the responsibility for the turn of events has at least been displaced from the whims of fortune to the power of love. "Oh wild and immense passion," moans Flaminia in the same monologue we have been commenting upon.[56] Nonetheless, what does emerge from this passage is a negative view toward fortune, attributing to its influence primarily life's adversities, as well as a clearer recognition of the human will as a force in life's triumphs. Accordingly, in the second segment quoted above, Flaminia, while deploring the thwarting of her ambitions, bitterly ascribes to Attila's acts of war, and her own subsequent readiness to fall in with Attila's plans, the cause of her frustration. Similarly, in a soliloquy in the final act, Flaminia comments on Celia's murder at the hands of Attila:

> So goes the world: one survives
> while the other writhes in pain;
> one person dies of a disdain,
> the other on it thrives.
> The poison which the king I gave
> this end has forward pressed;
> for him it has upset his breast,
> and I no longer need to rave.   (p. 109)

Although the first quatrain appears to describe the world's mutability as well as the counterbalancing of one person's happiness with another's misfortune, the second quatrain identifies Flaminia as the author of this state of affairs. In fact, the aphorism implicit in the first quatrain seems to find not only its illustration but its explanation in the second quatrain. That is to say that the state of the world as described generally in the first lines is the result of the behavior of people as described in the particular case of the next lines. Hermenegildo accurately perceives, as he cites from this play a courtier's lament on the rapid alternation of good and ill, that the "negative idea of fortune is one of the constants in Virués."[57] Our reading of these plays suggests that Virués was not only denigrating the influence of fortune but emphasizing the prominence of human volition in the course of events.

V *Summation*

In our attempt to apprehend the art of the four dramas discussed in this chapter, we have elected to concentrate upon fortune: how it (and the related concept of fate) is viewed; how it is contrasted with providence; what effect it is thought to have upon the course of human events; how its influence differs from that of human volition. In the course of this perusal, some other matters emerge. Most important, not only for the particular understanding of fortune in these plays, or for the general appreciation of Virués's dramaturgy, but for the pivotal position in the evolution of the Spanish drama which we have claimed for Virués, is the necessity to

The Response to Fate and Fortune

approach Virués's theater without the traditional insistence on subjecting the plays to the confining rules of tragedy. We shall return to this subject in the next chapter. For the moment it is important to bear in mind that our comprehension of the dramas is enhanced by our having permitted ourselves to study fortune and one's responses to it without a preconceived set of restrictions carried over from Classical precepts concerning the tragic hero, the kind of characters which make up tragedy, not to mention the conventional unities of action, time, and place. Conversely, by allowing such considerations to be set aside in order to appreciate the human attitude toward fortune, we have in this process come to see that these dramas do not fit the mold of Classical tragedy. To this point we shall also return in the next chapter.

Although we have nothing substantive to add to the question of the chronology of the plays beyond that which is summarized in our initial chapter, an interesting progression may be noted in the four plays studied in the present chapter. We cannot call this observation anything more than "interesting," for any conclusions which we might wish to draw would necessarily be based on not one but several related hypotheses. Froldi's suggestion, that *Elisa Dido* could belong to any period of Virués's productivity precisely because its Classical ambience and its five-act structure are atypical in comparison with the rest of Virués's dramas, remains valid in the absence of any contrary documentation. Froldi bases his supposition not only on the relative uniqueness of *Dido's* characteristics, but on Virués's own words in the prologue, in which the Valencian stresses the difference between this play and the other four. We could add in support of Froldi's conjecture that the fact that *Dido* is inserted at the end of the collection (with Virués's knowledge, since in the prologue he refers to it as the last) might at least counter the often-stated assumption that *Dido's* greater proximity to Classical imitation should make us consider it the first. But on both sides of this argument we tread on uncertain ground. Nonetheless, if we begin with *Dido* and follow the order of the present chapter — it will be recalled that Virués does explicitly identify *Semíramis* as the first of the others — we note a gradual decrease in the number of references to fortune. Moreover, as we have observed, by the time we reach *Attila* the nature of the references has shifted from an acknowledgment of life's ups and downs to a more limited recognition of fortune as the source of ill fortune. Stated another way, as we progress through the four plays, we note a decreasing dependence on fortune in general and a particular increase in the individual's ascribing to his or her own initiative the rise in status or the successful outcome of a plan. This is somewhat different from the medieval "conception that the rise and fall of empires depends not on desert ... but simply on the irresistible rough justice of Fortune, giving all their turns, [a conception which] did not pass away with the Middle Ages."[58] A rereading of our final quotation from *Furious Attila* above makes clear how Virués's conception takes the commonplace and makes it more dependent upon human machinations. Here, too, then, do we find in Virués an anticipation — albeit in a crudely constructed drama — of what was to come later, as Bradner has described it when he compares true Classical tragedies (in which "the hero is already [at the outset] caught in the trap") with the modern variety of "tragedy," so that "in Shakespeare, Marlowe, and Tirso [de] Molina, we watch the hero create his own tragic dilemma.... Tirso's sinner in *El condenado por desconfiado* (The Doubter Damned) does repent. These ... protagonists in Spanish and English tragedy actively work out their own fates within the compass of the play. They not only suffer; they prepare their own suffering."[59]

The concept of "fortune" approximates more and more the idea of "luck," which is to say that less thought is given to a divine power than to the deceptive and mutable nature of everyday life. In this world the dramatic possibilities lie, therefore, not in our being playthings of the gods but rather in our capacity to take advantage of the very instability of life which so confounds us. All of these matters find their greatest significance in Virués's *La infelice Marcela*, a play for which we have reserved a chapter apart.

CHAPTER 4

Marcela

LA infelice Marcela (Unhappy Marcela) deserves a place of its own for a number of reasons. These should become clear as we proceed with an examination of the play itself, but a summary of what others have said will not only provide an appropriate introduction but should explain why, in our insistence upon seeing Virués as a pivotal figure in the evolution of the Spanish *comedia,* this play above all others leads us to see Virués not as a tragedian but as a dramatic poet intuitively anticipating what greater talents — notably Lope de Vega — would shape into a national art form. This is not to suggest that we should bestow upon Virués such titles as "creator," nor that we should discern in Virués's plays the origins of the Spanish national theater. Some of the seeds of the later *comedia* are indisputably present, and for this Virués should be given appropriate credit. What is more to the point, however, is that in his efforts are reflected the yearnings of a hundred other poets, some of whom would earn fame and some of whom would fade into obscurity, but with most of whom Virués shared the desire to shape a dramatic art that, while retaining some of the elements of previous modes, would be more appropriate to the sensibilities of the epoch and the nation in which Virués lived and wrote. (That he lived and wrote elsewhere as well serves to explain, not diminish, the nature of his contribution.)

I *A Significant Ambivalence*

As we examine the judgments made by scholars we note a curious — and, therefore, interesting — inconsistency. Our analysis of *Unhappy Marcela* will be more meaningful if we first review this inconsistent attitude toward Virués's dramatic works, for much of the required clarification of the ambivalent assessment of Virués will enable us to appreciate the apparent ambiguities of *Marcela.*

We have used words like "inconsistency," "ambivalence," and "ambiguity." This is not equivalent to speaking of varying interpretations, which one would expect to find in the analyses of most artistic works. In our chapter one we alluded to the inconsistency: scholars have generally approached Virués's dramas with an eye for appraising them as tragedies. (Part of this is attributable to Virués's having labeled them as such. As we have seen, Lope de Vega himself described his *El castigo sin venganza* as a *tragedia* written "in the Spanish manner, and not in the manner of Greek antiquity and Latin severity."[1] Yet it is the exception, not the rule, to examine Lope's plays as though they were potential tragedies, regardless of how he chose to label them.) The inconsistency, then, is the classification of Virués's works as tragedies while proceeding to find fault with them for their failure to adhere to the characteristics of tragedy. Thus the previously cited work by Hurtado and Palencia dismisses all the plays but *Dido,* which is "the least defective of them." Since the specific word "defective" suggests not so much a negative evaluation of intrinsic worth as it does a process of finding faults measured against a scale of requisite ingredients, we need to be certain what such a scale is intended to measure. There is something "wrong," such assessments would have us believe, and the yardstick presumably is the set of distinctive features by which we define tragedy.

The above explains the inconsistency we encounter in Ticknor. Referring to Virués's plays aside from *Dido,* he categorically states, "All four of them are absurd."[2] As for *Dido,* it is "better," Ticknor says, but "it lacks a good development of the characters, as well as life and poetical warmth in the action; and being, in fact, an attempt to carry the Spanish drama in a direction exactly opposite to that of its destiny, it did not succeed."[3] The inconsistency we have been observing is once more at work. At first blush it would appear a strange position indeed for a literary historian to single out a work as better than others by the same author and then describe it as lacking good character development as well as life in the action. To include the criticism that it lacks "poetical warmth" would tend to divest it of any merit that might be left to it. This assessment is representative of many standard works. Yet, Ticknor's judgment is followed by a most interesting observation. Virués's work, or at least *Elisa Dido,* is described as an attempt to take the Spanish drama in a direction exactly opposite to that for which it was destined. If what is meant here is Virués's intention to write in the vein of Classical tragedy, then presumably it is for this reason that *Dido* is "better" in spite of the not insignificant artistic faults which are ascribed to it. Yet, if Virués *did not succeed,* as Ticknor maintains, was it because his attempts at tragedy did not succeed, or was it because Virués was instinctively heading in some other direction, indeed that direction which Ticknor labels "that of its destiny," which is to say *not* tragedy?

Such inconsistencies are not rare, as we have already suggested. Accordingly, we are not singling out some ill-conceived judgment as a "straw man," but rather have cited the above in order to present a widely held reaction to Virués's theater. Somewhat more intriguing are evaluations which, rather than inconsistent, we might call ambiguous. Illustrative of this approach is the observation by Bouterwek that "some of Virués' tragedies might almost be called *comedias.*"[4] More curious, perhaps, is Sargent's suggestion: "Perhaps it was well that he [Virués] did drop drama, for by the time he had written *Marcela,* though he had gained in technique, he was approaching too closely current concepts to make any startlingly original contributions to its development."[5] Sargent goes on to make the following observations in the concluding portion of her book:

The field where [Virués] excelled, where he is indeed unique, is in *Elisa Dido.* One might wish that he had been a little less versatile, that he had continued his energies upon developing it, rather than scattering them in the varying adaptions of classic drama represented by the other four plays. Yet it is perhaps a foolish wish.... And after all, Virués' actual contribution to the drama which did develop came from the other four plays — the use of three acts, and the adaptation of plots from every available source. We may decry lack of unity in the inspiration of Virués.... Yet what more characteristic of the drama of the *Siglo de Oro* than just such diversity of interests?[6]

The ambiguity of the above reflects praise of *Dido* for its Classical attributes while recognizing the ingredients of the Spanish *comedia* as Virués's "actual contribution to the drama which did develop." Not unlike this assessment is the more recent one by Ruiz Ramón, who describes Virués as "one of the most gifted for tragedy." He goes on to say that Virués's idea of tragedy is mistaken (*equivocada*), and then observes: "With each work, as he progresses in his productivity, he allows himself greater liberties in the structure of the tragedy until, in *Unhappy Marcela,* he blends the tragic with the comic. Although he calls it tragedy, this play no longer is one."[7]

With this perceptive commentary we have shifted from an ambiguity to a significant ambivalence. Although some of Ruiz Ramón's reasoning presupposes a chronological development from *Dido* to *Marcela* (these plays framing the three others), it is not dependent upon such a chronology. What does emerge is a recognition that *Marcela* is not a tragedy, and that *Marcela* allows such a perception to be clearly expressed. (Consider Hermenegildo's retort to Montiano's failure to discern the nature of *Marcela:* "How far the eighteenth-century critic was from understanding Virués's intention! Montiano wanted to fit this work into the mold of tragic precepts, when *Marcela* is no pure tragedy.")[8] Froldi has gone even farther. The Italian scholar suggests that the presence of "many elements" shows Virué's works to be "removed from the theoretical rigor of tragedy. This is noticeable especially in *Cruel Cassandra* and *Unhappy Marcela,* called tragedies only because of their unhappy endings, but which are characterized by an intrigue and by characters that will be typical of *comedias.*"[9] Crawford had earlier made a similar observation, but had limited these remarks to *Marcela:* "The play, to be sure, ends tragically, but the atmosphere is that of a romance of chivalry, far removed from the horrors of his earlier compositions."[10]

We have used the word "ambivalence," but modified by "significant," inasmuch as we do not intend "ambivalence" to be understood in a pejorative context, for although the word connotes hesitation, it has as well a simpler meaning, namely that it reflects the simultaneous attraction of opposing values. In other words, there is no need to state that some of the critics are "wrong" and others "right," for the fluctuating attitudes correspond to whether any or all of Virués's plays are to be evaluated within a tragic tradition or — and here is the critical point — as an intuitive effort in a period of political, cultural, and, specifically, poetic transition. This is to say that we need insist neither on Virués as a tragic poet nor on Virués as an innovator. Not only are scholars' comments about him ambivalent; Virués's own works display a significant ambivalence. Froldi, for instance, is one of the few to note not only the existence but the importance of a secondary plot in the very work (*Elisa Dido*) which is generally accepted as most nearly approximating Classical (or neo-Aristotelian) concepts, including the unities. Even in that work, then, Virués reveals an intention —

conscious or otherwise — of departing from the rigidity of the preceptists.

In a brief reference to Virués as "another writer of Senecan tragedy admired by Lope," Trueblood discusses the bringing of the chorus into dialogue with the characters and observes that both Virués and Jerónimo Bermúdez (1530?-1605?) were "eclectic dramatists."[11] Despite the intended focus upon only a single aspect — the chorus — Trueblood's observation may be extended to a more general evaluation of our poet, not unlike the ambivalence we have been noting. Perhaps more interesting is the development of Valbuena Prat's thinking, beginning with his early comment that the entire portion of the secondary plot "is almost superfluous,"[12] with no apparent recognition of the significance of that secondary action in *Elisa Dido*. More recently, Valbuena has called Virués "the most patent case of the fusion, successful to a greater or lesser extent, of 'classicism' or 'ancient art' — especially learned from Seneca — and of the 'free way' of those who shut up the precepts under lock and key."[13] Valbuena's recognition of Virués's pivotal role or, as he calls it, of the "fusion" of the traditions of what went before and what was to come, is the clearest statement of Virués and his place in the evolution of the Spanish drama. The question of innovation or originality, on the one hand, or of Classicism on the other, becomes subordinate in interest as well as importance to the ambivalent or pivotal posture we have insisted upon. Such a posture not only helps us to apprehend the work of Virués (the immediate purpose of this book) but to comprehend the ambience in which still greater artists and their art would flourish (the ultimate purpose of any humanistic investigation).

The foregoing has embraced Virués's theater in a general way. Scholars of different centuries and differing persuasions appear to share a common reaction which at first blush suggests inconsistency or ambiguity. Yet, when these views are placed in juxtaposition, a significant ambivalence emerges which reveals Virués in his pivotal position. As we review these comments, we discern, almost in the manner of a refrain, references to *Unhappy Marcela* underlying the observations of those who see in Virués's dramatic works a progressively more evident tendency to depart from (not rebel against) the content as well as the form of the Classical drama. We come, then, to the work which most obviously put that tendency in the foreground. We will note that its characteristics explain many of the features of the other four plays. Conversely, many of those features will help us to understand what otherwise would remain puzzling in *Unhappy Marcela.*

II *The Plot*

Princess Marcela of England, on her way to rejoin her husband, Prince Landino of León, is caught in a shipwreck off the coast of Galicia not far from Santiago de Compostela. Count Alarico, charged by Landino with the protection of Marcela, is nonetheless attracted by Marcela's charms and makes plain his intention to make love to the princess. Tersilo, another noble, attempts to dissuade Alarico from this dishonorable and treacherous behavior and, in an ensuing skirmish, Tersilo is mortally wounded.[14] Marcela turns for protection to a shepherd who has witnessed the fight, but the latter flees in fright, leaving Marcela at Alarico's mercy. As Alarico presses his suit, the action is interrupted by the appearance of a robber band. Alarico flees and Formio, leader of the bandits, goes after him, leaving Marcela in the hands of his lover, Felina.[15] Subsequently, Oronte, lord of a nearby castle, rescues Marcela, whereupon Felina vows vengeance.

In the second act, Landino appears in the Galician mountain country, having climbed on foot after his arrival on horseback. (These realistic details, quite unlike Virués's other plays, are provided not in stage directions but, as would be typical of the national *comedia,* communicated by the text of the play itself.) As he looks out to sea in hopes of espying a ship, he suggests to his men that they return to their horses and move on to Santiago, where he may await Marcela. Some shepherds, having overheard some of the conversation, realize that the captive Marcela is the princess, wife of Landino, and plan to aid the prince, primarily because of their own subjugation by the bandits whom they unwillingly serve. Meanwhile, the bandits have captured Alarico, and Felina is immediately attracted to him. Formio similarly falls in love with Marcela, who earlier had been recaptured. (Situations such as these prompted Valbuena Prat to speak of Virués's offering "a plot in which Lope de Vega would have moved as on his own ground.")[16] Felina overhears Formio's declarations of love to Marcela and Formio overhears a similar exchange between Felina and Alarico, whereupon each of the lover bandits plots to poison the other.

In the third act, Landino, with the help of the shepherds, manages to overpower the robber band in the cave where the bandits were encamped. Marcela, in the meantime, had begged Formio not to seduce her and to avenge her dishonor instead by killing the traitor Alarico. Formio leaves her alone, and Marcela, during a soliloquy centering upon the vicissitudes of life, drinks a beverage and eats a pastry which Formio and Felina, respectively, had prepared and poisoned for one another. Landino breaks in, but too late, for the poison has worked its effect and Marcela is dead, as are the bandits as a result of the attack upon the cave. Landino laments Marcela's death and amid an atmosphere of grief carries away the body of his dead wife with the help of the shepherds. With the final lines pronounced by "Tragedia," the play comes to a close.

III *Notable Elements*

Leaving aside for the moment any interpretations we may make of this work, we should take note of some features of *Unhappy Marcela* which not only aid such interpretations but in themselves constitute elements worth remarking upon. Of significance and interest is the generally accepted observation that this play is the first in which the *romance* form of versification is found.[17] For those not familiar with this characteristically Spanish strophic form, Wilson's summary serves as a concise description: "The *verso de romance,* or ballad meter, is the most thoroughly national of all Spanish meters, and was a popular form with the dramatists and poets of the Golden Age. It has maintained its popularity down to the present day. The lines are octosyllabic rhyme, have a single assonance throughout the passage...."[18] The importance of the appearance of the *romance* form in the Virués play lies less in its potential analysis as an innovation than in its reflection of Virués's sensibilities. Well in advance of the popularity of this meter in the national *comedia,* Virués intuitively sensed the compatibility of the strophic configuration of the national ballads and the evolving national theater. This in itself reveals an artistic consciousness of moving away from past models — whether of Classical or Italian forms, or of tragic tone and severity — and, given the absence of this meter in his other plays, reinforces our image of Virués as a pivotal figure.

With respect to the two possibilities for the utilization of metric alternation in general, namely, conformity with the character of the speaker or conformity with the character of the situation, Virués chose the latter, "and once more Lope was to follow suit."[19] Hermenegildo similarly notes that in *Unhappy Marcela* Virués "uses meters according to the character of the episodes: octaves in the soliloquies, *quintillas* in love scenes, blank verse and *romances* for narrative."[20] Once more, it is not a case of insisting on chronological priority, much less of innovation; we should, however, take note of these features as being in consonance with the evolving dramatic art in Spain.

It is difficult to understand Hermenegildo's comment that *Marcela* is "the tragedy which moves farthest away from Virués's usual style" (*común estilo*).[21] Leaving aside the nomenclature, which we have discussed earlier and which Hermenegildo accurately analyzes in subsequent paragraphs, it becomes more than a matter of statistics when we bear in mind that aside from the work in question, we possess no more than four plays by Virués, and of those it is generally agreed that *Elisa Dido* is largely dissimilar from the rest. Accordingly, the concept of a *común estilo* in the five dramas appears elusive, particularly in view of Hermenegildo's subsequent statement about *Marcela:* "The style of the work is the normal one in Virués...."[22] What does emerge, and Hermenegildo himself has put it clearly, is once more the pivotal nature of Virués's dramaturgy. In his earlier book of 1961, as well as in the more recent work published in 1973, Heremengildo noted that "Virués remained in an interesting stage, floating between a classicism which was slipping from his hands and a horrific 'novelesque' theater, imported from a decadent Seneca by way of Italy."[23] In the dozen years between these volumes, Hermenegildo has had occasion to ponder further, as the subsequent quotation following the sentence just cited reveals: "But let us understand well this 'interesting' situation of Virués.... It [the situation] must have been much less attractive for him, who found himself shoved aside by the masses.... At the same time, and this is the principal characteristic of Virués's vital way, our tragedian yielded to the pressures of the masses — the evolution of his theater, from *Elisa Dido* to *Unhappy Marcela* proves it — and he remained swimming among the waters in a difficult equilibrium which, if it played a role in the formation of the national theater, must have caused him more bitterness than happiness."[24]

Whether Virués truly felt bitterness as a result of the popular development of the Spanish theater remains conjectural (although he did prefer the approval of the elite, as we shall note in chapter 5).

Of interest as well is the shift in Hermenegildo's imagery with respect to what he terms Virués's "interesting" situation. If Virués was earlier viewed as "floating," a more active role is given to him in the subsequent vision of him "swimming." At any rate, the fundamental observation by Hermenegildo should not be passed over: he speaks of the *evolution* of Virués's theater, a process which is at once reflected in all the five dramas — even *Dido* introduces a secondary action — and which reaches its closest approximation to the formula of the coming national theater in the *Marcela*. It is in such a context that the inclusion of the *romance* form in particular, and the association of metric change with situational change in general, assume their major importance.

In the present volume we have not dealt with sources for the plays because these have been extensively described in Sargent's book. With respect to *Marcela,* however, we should emphasize, as Sargent has shown (pp. 102-109), that much of the plot of the Virués play is derived from cantos 12, 13, 20, 23, and 24 of Ariosto's *Orlando Furioso*. As with the matters discussed above, what is important for us here is neither the lack of originality that such adaptation might imply, nor the possible innovative nature of turning to Italian rather than Classical sources. In this, Virués was not the first (although he may be counted among the earliest),[25] but more significantly, neither was he among the last, by which we mean to stress how typical it would soon become of most writers to seek source material in the Italian epics and *novelle*. Accordingly, just as we noted elements of Tasso's *Gerusalemme Liberata* in Virués's *Monserrate,* so we note in *Marcela* a debt to Ariosto's *Orlando*. As Arróniz has noted, "equally as important [as the *Gerusalemme*] for the life of the Spanish *comedia* was the *Orlando Furioso* of Ariosto, from which Lope de Vega alone extracted themes for three *comedias*...."[26] To repeat: that Virués did this earlier is not in itself as significant as is the appreciation such a fact gives us for Virués's apprehension of what would later be called the new art of composing *comedias*. Referring to Virués's use of the *Orlando* for his *Marcela,* Sargent (p. 105) observes that although "pastoral tales had long enjoyed dramatic form both in Italy and in Spain, the use of chivalric poetry as a source of tragic plot appears to be new." We may debate whether it was indeed new and whether it is truly used here for a tragic plot,[27] but what becomes increasingly clear with each element examined is the approximation to the characteristics of the national theater. As Sargent (p. 109) points out: "Certainly *La infelice Marcela* approaches much more nearly than any other play of Virués the romantic comedy that was soon to outshine all else."

There remains another element to be noted. Sargent (p. 106), thinking particularly of Formio and Felina, comments that "here, for the only time, [Virués] has introduced characters outside the ranks of nobility." Hermenegildo similarly concludes that "Virués, for the first time in his theater, introduces plebeian characters beside nobles."[28] I have suggested elsewhere that there is good reason to believe that Formio and Felina may well have been of noble — possibly royal — blood.[29] If that argument is valid, further reflection suggests a new consideration of Virués's conception of what he labeled *tragedia*.

A close reading of the play reveals, as my cited article details, that Formio enjoyed royal rank and that Felina, perhaps of noble blood as well, was instrumental in Formio's downfall, whereupon they took to the life of banditry. Hermenegildo, who goes so far as to call Felina a prostitute, is not so severe with Formio, despite the latter's evident parallel behavior. (That this may be a reflection of the notorious "double standard" in such matters is immaterial.) What Hermenegildo does discern in Formio is the "curious" bifurcation of his manner of expression, at once forceful and brusque yet, in matters of love, the same as that which a typical Renaissance gentleman would use.[30] In addition to lending support to my own conclusion with respect to Formio's origins, the entire "prehistory" (in the sense that it does not, properly speaking, belong to the action contained in the play itself), is in accord with Hermenegildo's own thesis with respect to Virués's portrayal of court intrigue, the (moral) fall of rulers caught in their own lasciviousness as the result of women who corrupt them. To this we must add what we have found to be of importance in another context: the revelation of Semíramis's plebeian origins, specifically, the daughter of a prostitute. Hermenegildo comes close to sensing a parallel *in character* when, in an insightful comment on Felina's personality, he says that she is "the most complex and most forceful character" of the play. At times, continues Hermenegildo, Felina reminds him of the "ferocity of Semíramis, with a good dose of *popularismo*."[31] Unfortunately, he does not develop the analogue, but he does have occasion to describe a time in the course of the play when "Felina feels herself queen of the robber band...."[32]

Marcela

As we look more closely at the two plays, a parallel emerges which sheds some light on Virués's conception of his art. The *Semíramis* play presents the rise of a commoner, daughter of a whore, through soldier's wife, king's wife (queen), monarch (queen disguised as king), to ultimate fall at the hands of her own son (a product of her lust and no less immoral than the mother he resembles). Throughout the play lasciviousness and depravity are the dominating motifs. In *Marcela,* Felina is proud to declare that she is "Felina, the one who is wont to overturn a lineage, a kingdom, a world" (p. 127). Even in the scene in which Felina, considering Marcela her personal prisoner, orders the princess to disrobe and exchange clothes with her, we may discern a parallel with Semíramis's repeated change of dress, including the donning of her son's princely robes. Sargent (p. 106) interprets this scene in *Marcela* in a way quite opposed to Hermenegildo's insight into Felina's character:

The fact is, Virués is here straying from the course he seems to have laid out for himself.... The scenes in which Felina wrangles with Marcela over her clothes and the lost jewels, and nags Formio to get after Oronte, certainly approach comedy of manners; and we have comedy's time-honored situation of eavesdropper who hears ill of himself when she spies on Formio and Marcela and hears [herself described as "that crazy woman / whom I have in my company / whom I once did love, / and nevermore can love"].

Sargent's evaluation is accompanied by a footnote on the same page in which she maintains that humor is inherent in Felina's character. Although we have rather consistently agreed with the careful analyses of Virués's works that Sargent presents, we must differ on the interpretation of the scene in question as well as of the characters involved. If on other occasions in other plays we have argued that tragedy and a tragic hero were absent, so here we must insist that neither comedy nor humor is a significant feature of *Unhappy Marcela,* particularly not in the scene in question. (One may indeed point to some "comic" elements in the play, such as the cowardly shepherd mentioned in our summary of the first act, but the significance of that behavior lies not in its potentially risible nature, for it represents the refusal of Marcela's last plea for help and it abandons her to first Alarico and subsequently, the robber band.) Moreover, we can scarcely consider as comic the scene in which Felina exchanges clothes with Marcela. We are not led to concentrate on the potential humor of a bandit donning the finery of a princess; rather, we focus on the degradation and humiliation of Marcela. This element, then, which we have chosen to include among those in our section titled "Notable Elements," namely, the juxtaposition of persons of supposedly plebeian and noble origins, reflects a significance which transcends the apparent novelty itself.

IV Virués's Protagonists

Not only have we said that the elements discussed above would aid our interpretation of *Marcela;* we have also suggested that a separate look at *Marcela* would aid us in our appreciation of Virués's theater generally. The topic discussed above, namely the inclusion of apparently plebeian characters next to those of the nobility, both in principal roles, is one that deserves further comment. It is, as the critics have noted, in *Unhappy Marcela* that this element comes to the fore; it is, however, of more importance and it is not restricted to this one play. (It is, of course, necessary to bear in mind — though hopefully unnecessary to insist — that we are speaking of such a juxtaposition for those who play *major roles;* the mere appearance of people of humble origins alongside those of the nobility is hardly a matter worth pursuing.)

We have noted that Sargent sees the inclusion of Formio and Felina as the introduction of such plebeian elements ("for the only time") and that Hermenegildo agrees ("for the first time"). The former goes on to find comic elements in at least Felina; the latter finds Felina a complex and forceful character, reminiscent of no less than Semíramis (though tempered by *popularismo*), while expressing surprise at the elevated style of language which Formio is capable of using on occasion. McKendrick voices some bewilderment as she says of Felina that "she is important in that she is the first known example of a female bandit in the Spanish drama.... Although she refers to a past of violence and outlawry ... and although she lives with bandits, we are not told why she has become a bandit and she seems not to play an active part in the criminal life of the gang.... In the present play the extraneous references seem to have been introduced only to lend a rather naive ferocity to her character. She is essentially a bandit's moll — she even retains her feminine skirts — and her claims to infamy in her own right merely lend a little superfluous surface drama."[33] As one might expect, given our comments in the previous section, our own analysis of Felina attaches more importance to the allegedly extraneous references. We need not, however, insist upon noble blood for Formio and Felina for what follows.

Hermenegildo, as we have observed, puts forth a most interesting thesis which, although it remains uncorroborated also remains intriguing. (As noted earlier, it deals with the court corruption and intrigue and the undoing of the monarch.) Our purpose here is neither to support nor to refute this engaging interpretation, particularly insofar as it may or may not reflect Virués's views of the political situation of the second half of the sixteenth century. Nonetheless, as we proceed to discuss the nature of Virués's protagonists in the paragraphs below, it may be of help to keep in mind the basic interpretation — from the literary, if not the sociopolitical standpoint — which Hermenegildo proposes.

Leaving aside *Elisa Dido*,[34] a pattern emerges as we note a significant distinction between the reigning monarch (at least as the curtain rises, for the throne changes hands on a number of occasions!) and the person or persons who are the true prime movers of the events in the plays. That pattern is the portrayal of someone *other* than the original monarch as the protagonist or protagonists of the play. (We are using the word "protagonist" in its etymological sense of "one who contends for the first prize," rather than in the sense in which Frye, among others, distinguishes between "two main characters, a protagonist or hero, and an antagonist or enemy."[35] The distinction, although valid in many circumstances, could not easily be applied to most of the situations in Virués's plays — although it does apply to the *Monserrate* — as readers of our plot summaries will agree.) It is Cassandra, not the (significantly) anonymous prince and princess, much less the equally anonymous and far weaker king, who is the major source of the complications of the plot in *Cruel Cassandra*. It is Flaminia, not Attila, who drags the characters to their downfall in *Furious Attila*. It is Semíramis, not King Nino, who makes playthings of generals and kings throughout *Great Semíramis*. And now, in *Unhappy Marcela,* neither she nor her ineffective husband can control the course of events, which is determined by Alarico, Formio, and Felina. That all but Landino die (as do the protagonists of other plays) is less a moral lesson than a reflection of a fact of life and, in all likelihood, an indication of Virués's limitations with respect to how to bring a drama to a close. Whether we think of these works as misguided tragedies, or immature attempts at *comedias* (as that term is understood in Spanish), or possible essays in tragicomedy, it becomes clear as we reflect upon the dramatic situations in most of Virués's theater that we must distinguish between those who have been charged with ruling a kingdom or an empire on the one hand, and those whose personalities, machinations, and dynamism cause things to happen. If this seems evident now upon reflection, it is the rather special intervention of the bandits Formio and Felina in *Unhappy Marcela* that has permitted us to see the overall pattern of Virués's treatment of protagonists in his plays.

There is a larger context for an appreciation of Virués's handling of his subjects in this manner, as we discern from Hauser's commentary on the situation in the arts:

The feeling of insecurity explains the ambivalent nature of their [= artists and public] relation to classical art. The art critics of the seventeenth century had already felt this ambivalence, but they did not see that the simultaneous imitation and distortion of classical models was conditioned not by a lack of intelligence, but by the new and utterly unclassical spirit of the mannerists.

It was left to our own age, which stands in just as problematical relationship to its ancestors as mannerism did to classical art, to understand the creative nature of this style.... We are the first to grasp the fact that the stylistic efforts of all the leading artists of mannerism ... were concentrated, above all, on breaking up the all too obvious regularity and harmony of classical art and replacing its superpersonal normativity by more subjective and more suggestive features. At one time it is the deepening and spiritualizing of religious experience and the vision of a new spiritual content in life [cf. the *Monserrate*]; at another, an exaggerated intellectualism, consciously and deliberately deforming reality, with a tinge of the bizarre and the abstruse....[36]

And subsequently:

Motifs which seem to be of only secondary significance for the real subject of the picture are often overbearingly prominent, whereas what is apparently the leading theme is devalued and suppressed. It is as though the artist were trying to say: "It is by no means settled who are the principal actors and who are the mere walkers-on in my play!"[37]

Although the above is principally concerned with painting and sculpture, its relevance to the works of Virués needs no clarification. By an examination of the kinds of characters who play the dominant roles (particularly as opposed to their corresponding position in the social hierarchy which the drama depicts), what emerges may or may not reflect Virués's responses to the sociopolitical events during the reign of Philip II. What seems beyond dispute is the ineffectiveness of the sovereign in Virués's plays with respect to playing the leading role, unless an episode of usurpation led the character to the throne. The dramatic importance, accordingly, is found in the conflicts of socially inferior but more dynamic and resourceful individuals. (We are, of course, a long way from a true concern for the common people and it would be a serious error for us to suggest any such tendencies in Virués's works. For this reason, our interpretation of Formio and Felina as members of the nobility assumes an added importance.)

At the close of our chapter three we stated that in this world the dramatic possibilities lie not in our being playthings of the gods but rather in our capacity to take advantage of the very instability of life which so confounds us. Combining that observation with our remarks here about the dynamism and resourcefulness of the true protagonists of Virués's dramas, we note a greater consistency in Virués's concept of the theater than he has been given credit for.

V *Fortune Once More*

Two passages in this play deal specifically with the familiar theme of attributing to fortune the origin of one's change of circumstance. In the second act, Alarico bemoans his imprisonment by the bandits:

> In this way, miserable world?
> In this way, mutable fortune?
> First to the halo of the moon,[38]
> now to the depths I'm hurled?
> Yesterday grand lord above,
> today tormented slave?
> Yesterday lost for fear of waves,
> today now lost because of love!
> Yesterday lost there at sea,
> today lost more on shore!
> In this way, world, so by this war
> you're wont to treat your progeny?   (p. 131)

At first blush, the passage seems scarcely worthy of comment, so replete is it with commonplaces. The "miserable world" theme is not only a traditional complaint of mortals generally but one which pervades Virués's other plays. The vicissitudes of this life, apparent *leitmotiv* of the passage, also appears to be no more than the recurrence of a familiar theme. When we relate these matters to each other, then to the rest of the passage, however, and then relate that to the context of the play in which it is found, we find that we are dealing with a rather clear example of how fortune is *not* the capricious author of change that tradition enjoys portraying as such.

The reference to the world, in addition to the evident utilization of a conventionalism, is a clue for our understanding that Alarico is considering only that kind of fortune which we have come to recognize as *worldly* fortune. We have seen elsewhere that for Virués this distinction, although clearly grasped by his contemporaries, often required emphasizing *as a distinction*. But this dramatic work, unlike the narrative epic, does not permit the intrusion of the author. We must accordingly make our own distinction between Virués's viewpoint and that expressed by a character in the play. The nature of that character should therefore not be overlooked. What is it that is really being contrasted by Alarico? The apparent *ubi sunt* refrain does not ring true.

It is a fact, as Alarico's description of "today" emphasizes, that his current predicament is not a felicitous one. Yet there is a curious paradox contained in the "yesterdays" with which his present misery is compared. In contrast to today's abyss, yesterday saw him as high as the moon; in contrast to today's slavery, yesterday he was a grand lord. Yet, yesterday embraces as well the fear caused by the storm at sea, the sense of perdition during the shipwreck, disasters which are compared — rather than contrasted — with today's fear caused by love and the resultant perdition on land. If we seem to be moving from one commonplace to another — we now have met another dominant theme in Virués's works, namely, the power of love — we should not lose sight of why love's potency has caused not merely the usual pangs but no less than perdition. A few lines below those included in our quotation, Alarico makes plain the dishonorable nature of his behavior toward Marcela, twice suggesting that his present grief is well deserved, stressing that it was he who brought injury and infamy upon "the princess, Landino, my honor, the just heavens" (p. 131). Accordingly, Alarico's almost conditioned response to adversity by blaming fortune and a similar reaction to the lust as caused by the god of love, is tempered by the recognition that he caused his own disgraceful disloyalty by his behavior. Moreover, by his comprehension of the justness of his punishment, Alarico is unwittingly recognizing not worldly fortune with its gratuitous gyrations, but divine retribution as a result of his own admitted disregard for his monarch, his own honor, and heaven itself. In short, Virués presents man as the transgressor, in contradistinction to man as the hapless victim of fortune's whims.

Of a different order is the third-act soliloquy pronounced by Formio following a discussion with his men:

> Oh barbaric, common, lowly lot,
> mother of rebellions and upheavals,
> daughter of the wild plebeian smut,
> fury which begets and nurses evils;
> varied, mutable, fickle, lacking gut,
> seeking goals that can but be ills,
> what celestial forces and what influence
> causes in men so great a difference?

Following a strophe which expresses his wonder at the difference in intelligence among individuals, Formio continues:

> Providence of heaven is it with which the earth
> supports itself in balanced weight and measure;
> I, second to none in the country of my birth
> in blood, honor, brains, and treasure;
> now see myself confused as to its worth
> when these varieties I weigh and measure;
> . . . .
> Who can stand up, who can be strong,
> against what heaven can desire or permit?
> In the end death, equalizer, will come along
> and take me where heaven deigns me to admit,
> while I the death of my Felina do conspire
> so it may come when I plot my desire.   (p. 139)

Not only are the language and the imagery indicative of a nobler birth than Formio's status as a bandit would imply, but the autobiographical elements contained in this soliloquy lead us to view Formio as something other than a commoner. Our reaction to his philosophical musings, therefore, becomes one of more seriousness than might have been expected, had we instead continued to believe that we were privy to the incongruous notions of a greedy bandit. The distinction which Formio perceives and articulates between his own intelligence and that of his band serves not only to distinguish him from those around him, but leads naturally to an observation about the different attributes of individuals. (Once more we note the characteristic progression from the particular circumstance to the general principle.)

As Formio ponders the cause of the inequitable and perplexing distribution of personal characteristics among humans, Virués once again aids our comprehension by having Formio clarify that we are now dealing not with worldly fortune but divine providence. Matters such as intelligence are not subject to the ups and downs of mundane mutability. Attributes of this sort are in the unfathomable domain of "celestial forces," and the contrast between this factor as a determining force in the behavior of men and the worldly attributes of birth and station is reflected not only in Formio's rhetoric but, as in the case of Alarico earlier, through our understanding of the character in the play. Whether we wish to insist upon Formio as a bandit or whether we accept him as of noble birth, he understands that intelligence — employed here as an example, not as a unique exception — is of a God-given origin. Yet his *behavior* obeys the similarly God-given free will. This explains Formio's confusion, whereas Virués, of course, remains consistent: the inexorability of death and its equalizing character are once again commonplaces which serve to put in relief the more significant message contained in the last lines of the passage quoted. The *dramatic* interest — as opposed to the exposition of philosophical truths — lies in what humans do about their circumstance while on this earth and in this life. (Virués's frequent references to *this* world, *this* life, and *this* age imply the existence of *another* world, *another* life, and *another* time. They also tend to make us focus on the conflicts *here;* hence, they stress the drama of this world.) Accordingly, while Formio muses about the inevitable and egalitarian nature of death generally, he reverses the previous direction of his thinking by returning to the particular circumstance — that is to say, situations over which he may in fact exert his will — and thereby limits his concerns to the temporal matters of human conflict: while he recognizes that ultimately providence controls life and death, *in the meantime* he will plot Felina's murder by poison.

The two passages discussed above complement one another. Alarico comments on worldly fortune; Formio ponders the inscrutability of divine providence. Although each appears to blame the respective variety of fortune for his predicament, both individuals implicitly accept the responsibility for their behavior in this world. The deeper we penetrate the references to fortune, the more evident is the superficiality of the supposed belief in its potency. This deliberate handling of the theme of worldly fortune may help to explain what otherwise could be passed over as mere theatrical devices — often clumsy ones at that — such as the overhearing of a supposedly private conversation by a third character ensconced in an unlikely hiding place. The second-act dialogue between Formio and Marcela, for instance, is overheard by Felina. It is the passage in which Formio expresses his love for Marcela and his declaration (cited earlier) that he can never again love Felina. It is, therefore, the passage which sets in motion so much of the ensuing intrigue, including the ultimate poisoning of Marcela. Having overheard Formio's declarations, Felina asserts: "Remarkable stroke of luck it has been to overhear this speech" (p. 135). But was it luck?

Felina is a jealous woman. In the very passage under consideration, Formio complains that he is ever under her watchful eye. Yet only moments before, he had told Felina to leave him alone with Marcela "for a certain plot which I need to weave" (p. 134). After only enough time for Formio to speak eight lines to Marcela, Felina makes her stealthy reappearance, stating her motive for eavesdropping: she has, she tells us, a certain suspicion. As the conversation between Formio and Marcela proceeds, Felina tells us that she is under no illusions, for her suspicion has been verified. It stands to reason that we, the audience, were prepared for something like Felina's return to spy on Formio while he wished to weave his mysterious plot alone with Marcela. The eavesdropping is consistent with Felina's character and so it is scarcely "luck" that has allowed her to overhear the conversation. The gratuitous comment about luck can therefore be explained either as the typical inconsequential expletive it most likely is, or as one further instance in which a character attributes to chance something which he or she quite plainly brought about deliberately. In no event, however, may we discern in this statement a concession by Virués to the power of fortune as having set the stage — literally as well as figuratively — for the ensuing complications and outcome of the plot.

VI *Marcela's Death*

We have insisted throughout our study of Virués's dramatic

works that whatever value we may wish to bestow upon his or his contemporaries' use of the term *tragedia,* we should not attempt to force his works — even *Elisa Dido* — into a rigidly Classical framework. It would seem to follow, and even scholars who seek tragedy in Virués's works generally agree, that of all the plays, *Marcela* is the least likely candidate for the category of tragedy, no matter what our perspective or definition may be. In what follows, we are not about to suggest that we should oppose all those who, like Froldi, Ruiz Ramón, and Hermenegildo, have accurately insisted that *Marcela* is not a true tragedy (not to mention those who have ridiculed this play because it does not conform to their conditioned definitions of tragedy). To find a perspective which may help us appreciate this work in particular, and Virués's evolving conception of dramatic art generally, it will be fruitful to focus on the ending, especially the death of Marcela.

It has been suggested that Marcela's death serves no purpose. Although she had expressed a desire for death on several occasions during her captivity as the only alternative to Formio's expressed intention to make her his wife (despite the fact that she was already married to Landino), her rescue was imminent, a fact she could not know but which the dramatist had planned and, with it, apparently eliminated any dramatic necessity for her death. Nonetheless, Marcela's death does serve to illustrate the vanity of mundane glories, the inexorability and unpredictability of death, as well as the increasingly important concept (for the Spanish drama of the time) that if one dies with honor death is not to be feared. There remains, however, another aspect.

In a study which, though debatable and somewhat controversial, raises some thought-provoking questions on tragedy in the *comedia,* Reichenberger reaches the following suggestive conclusions about Lope de Vega's *El caballero de Olmedo.* The question he addresses is whether or not this *comedia* ought to be considered a tragedy: "My answer will be just as ambivalent or ambiguous as so much of Spanish Baroque literature is: yes, on the human level, no, on the dogmatic level. Yes, because the splendid specimen of the perfect knight, maybe too innocent to live in this world, dies, destroyed by the base passions of *celos* [jealousy] and *envidia* [envy]. The words quoted before ['How little credit I gave to warnings from heaven! Trust in my own valor has decieved me'] indicate that it is his overly confident trust in his valor which made him disregard [the warnings from heaven]. The early happiness of his bride to be, Inés, is also doomed.... The same relationship can be formulated in Aristotelian terms: Don Alonso is an essentially good man, whose tragic flaw is too much self-reliance. The play ends not only with justice administered by the king, but also with a ray of hope.... Thus our yearning for belief in an orderly universe is satisfied."[39]

It is not, of course, our purpose here to debate the potential tragic nature of Lope de Vega's play, much less to become involved in the larger issue of whether tragedy exists at all in the Spanish drama of the Golden Age. What the quotation above allows us to do is to see a *correspondence* between tragic conceptions (not conventions) of the period we are considering, and those of an earlier (Classical) age which perhaps too inflexibly — among critics and theorists more than among creative authors — has persisted in remaining not only the prototype but the touchstone of tragedy. With the foregoing in the back of our mind, then, let us take a fresh look at Marcela's character and the interpretation of her death.

Scholars generally agree that Marcela is not a dynamic personality. Hermenegildo describes her as a "passive and insignificant character who greatly limits the possibilities of the totality. She shows herself to be more feminine than Cassandra or Semíramis."[40] Sargent (p. 107) calls Marcela "the ideal wife" and includes her among other characters who are "colorless." McKendrick similarly concludes that "Marcela — gentle, faithful and loving — is a colourless wraith in comparison [to the female protagonists of the other plays]."[41] If in the face of these remarks we paraphrase Reichenberger's analysis of Lope's hero, we find that Marcela may be viewed as a splendid specimen of the perfect lady, maybe too innocent to live in this world, who dies destroyed by the base passions of jealousy (the motive for the poisoning of the food and drink which she ultimately consumes) and envy (Felina's mockery of her royal status), as well as the omnipresent sexual desire of the men around her: Landino (legitimately), Alarico and Formio (illicitly). The earthly happiness of her husband is also doomed, which Sargent found remarkable because he does not die: the play "spares the hero, but he is with difficulty restrained from suicide!" (p. 143). The play ends with justice administered by the death of the bandits at the hands of Landino and his followers — poetic justice, we might add, since the followers are the very shepherds who had been forced to serve the bandits — and with a ray of hope: Landino successfully resists the despair of suicide and accepts

Ismenio's advice not to allow his prudence to be separated from his fortitude.[42]

It may be argued that we have stretched some points, in particular the suggestion that the base passions enumerated above contribute to the heroine's destruction, when of course these passions are those propelling the behavior of *others*. That it is her beauty or her very femininity that arouses such passions may, of course, be construed as Virués's peculiar tragic vision of women, since it is their sensuality which sets in motion so much of the intrigue in his theater, be it a perversity as manifest in a Semíramis or a virtue as displayed by a Dido or a Marcela. (In this respect, Virués's Marcela shares some characteristics with Cervantes's Marcela, whose beauty brought forth the despair of Grisóstomo.)[43] However, given the evolving Spanish *comedia* and its central concerns, it is more consistent to suggest that what may correspond to a "tragic flaw" in Marcela is her role as woman in an ambience where her honor and that of her husband is ever in danger and in which dishonor for a married woman inevitably leads to catastrophe. It goes without saying that this is not a flaw in Marcela's character, and for this reason we have insisted upon the notion of correspondence rather than equivalence. But if Reichenberger can discern such an element in Lope's character — too much self-reliance — a similar observation may be made of Marcela's reliance upon the honor inherent in the noble. To Alarico's improper advances she opposes his loyalty to his monarch and his own noble birth. Otherwise, her only alternative is death (p. 125). Significantly, she uses a similar argument to avoid seduction by Formio, for she has recognized nobility in the bandit leader:

> And you, sir, for it is but obvious,
> although you live in this abyss,
> that you have blood clear and illustrious,
> agree to show me love in this.
> Don't harm me, force me not;
> look who I am and who you are:
> for the love for me you say you've got,
> I ask that you your passion do debar. (p. 142)

Both Alarico and Formio — although neither is able to carry out the seduction — reply in similar terms: Alarico tells her it is useless "to wound the wind with voices" (p. 125); Formio refers to her

Marcela

"giving words to the wind" (p. 142).

It is following the exchange with Formio that Marcela unwittingly consumes the poison which Felina and Formio had prepared for each other. Not fate, but the base passions which are the motivating forces of the Spanish *comedia* lead Marcela to her death. But the *comedia* is moved as well by the countering forces of virtuous behavior. This dichotomy and the resultant dramatic conflict form the central concern of the national theater. Lope de Vega, in his *New Art,* asserted that

> honor cases are the best
> because everyone is forcefully moved by them,
> with them virtuous actions,
> for virtue is loved everywhere. (vv. 327-30)

The specific linking of virtue with actions reflects the dual sense of the word "virtue": in its modern sense as the antithesis of vice as well as in its etymological derivation from the same source which gave us "virility."[44] We do not mean to suggest by this last concept any connotations of masculinity, but rather the association of this word with the virtue of fortitude, applicable, it goes without saying, to women as well as men. Marcela, as all have been quick to point out, is scarcely a virile character and even the word "heroine" may seem forced. What needs to be emphasized, however, is that the dramatic situation — the "stuff" of drama — in which Marcela finds herself is precisely that which Lope de Vega would later describe as the "best" kind of situation: jeopardized honor in conflict with virtuous responses. We need not speak of tragedy, for the term is charged with controversy. Nonetheless, we may perceive a corresponding set of forces and conflicts in which the ladies and gentlemen of the Spanish *comedia* found themselves almost inevitably. Marcela's death is not a violent one. As she gradually and peacefully falls into eternal sleep, she remarks that everything can be tolerated, even death, so long as it has not been at the cost of chastity and honor (p. 143). The significance of this tranquil death lies, therefore, not in its interpretation as a punishment for wickedness. As Virués approaches the dramatic art which would soon be developed by others into a tradition of its own, his intuition has portrayed in the heroine not a new example of monstrosity but the model of virtue whom even Sargent dubbed "the ideal wife." Although Marcela's manner of resistance is a far cry from the heroic response of the women to be found, for example, in the *comedias* of Rojas Zorrilla (1607-1648),[45] the fact of her preserved chastity accounts for the untroubled nature of death. Tragedy, in the Classical sense, is not the appropriate way to describe this work, but tragedy finds its corresponding drama in what is best described by a word such as *problem*. (We have noted that Lope de Vega uses "cases" and this reflects a similar perspective.) The problem of acting virtuously while responding to a world in which honor is constantly threatened constitutes the drama of the Spanish Golden Age. Marcela, finding herself caught in this problem, makes the error of appealing to an adversary's nobility, when what is required is virtuous *action*. The elements of tragedy remain in this play, but the intrinsic nature of tragedy is already overshadowed by the need to respond not only with patience but with fortitude to the "honor cases."

CHAPTER 5

The Prologues and Epilogues

WE have left for last a consideration of the prologues and epilogues of Virués's works, not only because some of them — notably the prologue to the 1609 edition of his works, as well as the prologue to the *Monserrate* — clearly were composed after the completion of the works they were intended to introduce, but because they are so much more meaningful if we use them to consider the works retrospectively. With respect to what we have generically termed epilogues, these include as well the final recitation of a work by an allegorical figure not otherwise involved in the plot, inasmuch as the function of such closing statements is analogous to the *deus ex machina* effect of a formal prologue or epilogue, while still allowing the poet the artifice of having his thoughts spoken neither by himself nor by any of the *dramatis personae* whom the audience has come to know in a more concrete role. Final remarks spoken by allegorical figures, therefore, tend to reflect a sense that, although the fictional play has ended, the concluding statement is a disinterested statement of truth.

Although she is not referring to drama but poetry generally, Barbara H. Smith has observed that the "devices of closure often achieve their characteristic effect by imparting to a poem's conclusion a certain quality that is experienced by the reader as striking *validity*, a quality that leaves him with the feeling that what has just been said has the 'conclusiveness,' the settled finality, of apparently self-evident truth."[1] In his detailed study of prologues in the Spanish Golden Age as a literary genre in their own right, Porqueras Mayo notes that the epilogue "may have characteristics similar to those of the prologue, but differing from it by its specific distinctive function of 'non-introductoriness.'"[2] The apparent tautology serves to underscore the psychological distinction: in a prologue one expects to find clues with respect to what is yet to come; an epilogue, whether it adds something new or explains what has gone before, does not serve the purpose of preparing the audience. It is in the similar characteristics which, as Porqueras points out, prologues and epilogues share, that our interest lies. More so in the plays than in the epic, of course, the prologues and epilogues afford the poet the rare opportunity to intrude — to narrate, if you will — and add a third dimension to the plot-audience relationship. It is in this intrusion, then, and only secondarily in it as an introduction, that the prologue attracts our interest here, and it is in this same way that epilogues will concern us in this chapter.

I *The* Monserrate *Prologue*

We have already discussed the poet's intrusions and their purpose in the *Monserrate*. Because of its narrative structure, the ability of the author to intervene not only as storyteller but as discussant — though not in dialogue, for the characters do not respond — distinguishes his function here from that in the dramas. Accordingly, this prologue is of a nature somewhat removed from the prologues to the plays. Moreover, the difference in genre naturally signifies a difference in audience: in place of the drama's spectators and listeners *as well as* readers, Virués's epic, though potentially suitable for oral recitation (a tone it often assumes as it reflects its generic origins), is primarily intended to be read. Furthermore, unlike the prologues to the several plays, the prologue to the *Monserrate* is written in prose.

Before discussing this prologue, we should mention that each of the cantos of the poem is preceded by an octave in verse (sharing the strophic form of the total poem) called *argumento*. There are, accordingly, twenty such octaves, each providing an extremely concise summary of the plot of the canto to follow. As Porqueras points out (citing several examples), this type of argument often assumes the characteristics of a prologue. On the other hand, observes Porqueras, it is very common in the Golden Age for an *argumento* to be restricted to a "mere anticipatory summary without any liveliness of expression or contact with the reader."[3] Such is the case with the arguments preceding the individual cantos of the *Monserrate* and, therefore, they hold no further interest for us here. The prologue to the work itself, on the other hand, merits our translating it in its entirety:[4]

> The two parts with which poetry reaches its point of perfection (as its

two excellent masters, Aristotle and Horace, teach us) are sweetness and utility, and these must be borne in mind whenever anything is written in verse; but one must particularly strive for them, and with even greater care and diligence, in that paramount poetry called *epic* or *heroic,* which is that which, within the confines of a single action, forms a poem, such as the *Aeneid* of Virgil. Inasmuch as I wanted to compose a work in this poetic genre, taking for its action the miraculous appearance of the image of Our Lady of Montserrat and the founding of her holy house, it seemed to me that the first two parts could not fail me as far as subject was concerned; and so I determined to put into it the talent which God was kind enough to grant me, by whose grace I have come out with the present book. The zeal I have has been good, and with it I have used poetic invention in the part which the story as a human one has allowed it, which is that relating to the hermit Garín, attempting to paint him as a heroic and true Christian, with various digressions and examples which, without altering the history, should look to those previously cited principal aims of usefulness and pleasure. In the part of this poem which deals with the sacred image (preserving the respect and decorum due a matter of so much and so divine a quality), the poetry has done no more than tell the historical truth, with no more adornment than the verse requires, as will be seen in canto 18 and in the last one which, although Garín's relating it as if it were a prophecy is poetic invention, is in what he says pure truth. I wanted to point this out so that it will be understood that in dealing with the holy story that I took for the plot and basis of my poem I have maintained a Christian awareness as much as possible, just as in the poetry I have paid attention to the two parts I mentioned, sweetness and utility. If my book has attained the proper goal of all this, God be praised, and if not, so be it.

The familiar references to Aristotle and Horace, in addition to the conventionalism of the times with respect to the invocation of Classical models and authorities, constitute an acknowledgment of the principle of poetry as blending profit with delight, a concept specifically articulated by Horace in his *Ars poetica.* It is a commonplace in Golden Age literature — in practice as well as in theory — and Virués clearly incorporates it not only in the *Monserrate,* but in his plays as well. The mention of Aristotle is more readily linked with the problem of historical truth and poetic truth, a matter we have discussed earlier. Now that we are familiar with the poem and the legend it depicts, however, an intriguing question arises: did Virués know that the story of Garín was not factual?

The matter is of more than passing interest, for it bears on Virués's life as well as on his work. As we read the prologue to this religious epic, we are struck by its insistence on its — or, more significantly, its author's — Christian purpose. In itself, this avowal is not uncommon, particularly in the post-Tridentine period in which Virués lived. However, if Hermenegildo is correct in his suspicion that Virués was a *converso* (that is, that he was not of Christian ancestry), the prologue needs to be seen in a light other than the conventional explanation of a poet's theoretical musing. Hermenegildo goes so far as to suggest that the *Monserrate* "is a pretext for a self-presentation, in order to associate the first person [the "I" that Hermenegildo sees pervading Virués's works] with the thematic concern of the poem or, perhaps, the poem's thematic concern with the first person. That is why he gave us his portrait there."[5] This last point refers, of course, to the previously cited self-description in the poem. The hypothesis which Hermenegildo puts forward would help to explain not only why Virués described himself in the poem, but also would add a new perspective to the poet's intrusions into the action. Moreover, it goes without saying that the hypothesis, if correct, would explain why Virués chose to identify himself with the sinner turned saint. All of this, in turn, would serve to clarify the insistence upon — almost protestations of — the Christian awareness, Christian purpose, and fidelity to the truth of the sacred portions of the story, as expressed in the prologue. On the other hand, we may reach the same conclusions without the need to insist on what in those days was described with the unhappy term of "tainted blood." Precisely because of the tensions of the age on this point, tensions which led Américo Castro to refer to the period as an *edad conflictiva* —an age bristling with conflict — it was hardly a rarity for anyone, particularly those of learned and humanist backgrounds, to feel that tension and to deem it prudent to assert his Christianity.[6] In short, regardless of Virués's ancestry, his sensitivity on this issue most likely is the basis for the inordinate emphasis upon the Christian intent of a work that in any case is devoted to a miracle worked by no less than the Virgin Mary herself.

In view of the foregoing, we may now address the question raised previously. Since, as the most authoritative work on the history of Montserrat is eager to emphasize,[7] the entire story — not only the more imaginative elements — of the monk Garín is apocryphal, did Virués know this to be so or did he believe that there was at least some factual basis for the hermit's existence and his involvement in the founding of the monastery? Virués openly declares that it is in the part which deals with Garín that he has employed poetic invention. Yet, the various digressions and examples, which are included in order to adhere to the Horatian principle of profit and pleasure, do so, Virués is careful to tell us, *without altering the history.* Even if we recall that the history-story dichotomy had not yet taken hold (in modern Spanish they continue to be one word, although the concepts have, of course, long since been separated),[8] Virués seems to have some reason to point out that the matter of Garín — whether story or history — is not altered by the digressions. If Virués believes it to be history, the assertion remains interesting, but no more than that. If, on the other hand, Virués considers it merely a story, how are we to explain his insistence that he has not altered it?

It is here, then, that the allusion to Aristotle comes to our aid, and the subsequent reference to Virgil's *Aeneid* bears this out: since "poetic invention" is applied to that portion of the work which at the same time remains an unaltered *historia,* we are clearly in the area of the poetic universal. This aspect of the prologue is not unlike the opening paragraph of *Don Quixote,* published some two decades later: Cervantes feigns ignorance of his hero's name, adding that this "means very little so far as our tale is concerned; it is enough that in its narration we not depart one iota from the truth."[9] We now understand the repeated references in the *Monserrate* to Garín's being "worthy of poem and history." The poetic truth contained in the story of the monk, a legend which Virués appropriated for his poem, is accorded as much importance as the historical truth which Virués declares the miracle of the Virgin's image to be. The motive may indeed be Virués's status as belonging to a family of *conversos;* it may as well be a similar reaction to the *edad conflictiva;* it may just as well be the posture of a poet whose purpose was to insist that the poetic truth he had labored to present was every bit as worthy as the "history" around which it was woven. Our three suppositions do not leave the matter unresolved, for not only are they *not* mutually exclusive, but they share a common element: the poet's understanding of his art, an art in which the historicity of a subject is subordinate to its elaboration. It shall be worthy of poem *and* history. Here, once more, we observe the pivotal role of Virués, for alongside the ethical concerns of the sixteenth century (e.g., the post-Tridentine conception of fortune), we find a literary approach which is characteristic of the Middle Ages.

As C. S. Lewis has observed, in medieval literature many of the "vivid close-ups are not, as a whole, original. It is astonishing how often this occurs. One is tempted to say that almost the typical activity of the medieval author consists in touching up something that was already there; as Chaucer touched up Boccaccio, as Malory touched up French prose romances which themselves touched up earlier romances, as Layamon works over Wace, who works over Geoffrey, who works over no one knows what. We are inclined to wonder how men could be at once so original that they handled no predecessor without pouring new life into him, and so unoriginal that they seldom did anything completely new."[10] It was not a primary concern of the poets to be original with respect to subject matter: "Far from feigning originality, as a modern plagiarist would, they are apt to conceal it. They sometimes profess to be deriving something from their *auctour* at the very moment when they are departing from him."[11] Virués's prologue to the *Monserrate,* accordingly, combines this medieval attitude toward plot and subject matter with his own post-Tridentine preoccupations and a Renaissance concern for equating (aesthetically) the universal truths of poetry with the particular truths of history (not to speak of subordinating the latter to the former).

As is so often the case when one deals with conventions and traditions of this nature, we find in the literature generally, and at times in one and the same author, an antithetical strain developing alongside what otherwise might have seemed to be the prevailing attitude. (As we shall note below, Virués himself asserts his originality in other prologues, consistent with the pivotal posture we continually perceive in his works.) Curtius lists four typical categories for introductory passages of the sort we are considering here: (1) the topos "I bring things never said before"; (2) dedication; (3) the topos "The possession of knowledge makes it a duty to impart it"; (4) the topos "Idleness is to be shunned."[12] Commenting on these *topoi,* Porqueras Mayo concludes that "only the first enjoys any vogue in the Spanish Golden Age."[13] It is noteworthy, therefore, that this element is not among those found in the prologue to the *Monserrate.* On the other hand, "Christian authors like to present their works to God."[14] Given the speculation that exists concerning Virués's background, the final line quoted in our translation of this prologue may be more than a formula. (In point of fact, none of the other epic poems contained in the volume which we have been using as our source goes any further than to state [in the prologue] a wish that the benefactor to whom the work is dedicated be protected by God, or that the work will serve God.

The Prologues and Epilogues

Only Virués suggests that if his poem is successful, the glory should go to God [*la gloria sea a Dios*]. Although our translation has rendered this as the more conventional "God be praised," we should not lose sight of the potential relationship between a literal reading and Virués's need to be perceived as a Christian poet.)

II *The Prologue to the Plays*

Although the edition of Virués's works published in 1609 contains, as the title reveals, lyric poetry as well as the five dramas, the prologue to the *Obras trágicas y líricas del Capitán Cristóbal de Virués* (Tragic and Lyric Works of ... Virués) makes only a passing reference to the poems, concentrating instead on the plays.[15] The brief prologue, addressed to the "discreet reader," may be translated as follows:

> In this book there are five tragedies, of which the first four are composed by having attempted to bring together in them the best of ancient art and of modern custom, with the requisite order and attention so that it seems they reach the appropriate standpoint which theatrical works in our time ought to make use of. The last tragedy, of Dido, is all written in the style of the Greeks and Romans, with care and study. In all of them (although composed as a pastime, and in youth), there are set forth heroic and serious moral examples, as is appropriate to their serious and heroic style, and this intention is no less visible in the lyrical works, for they as well conform to the required point of mixing the useful with the sweet, as the author did in his book of Montserrat: read on happily.

Despite the greater concern for the plays, the prologue clearly views all the works contained in the edition as literature, that is, as works to be read. This is not surprising inasmuch as we are dealing with a prologue to a printed edition (Virués himself refers to it as "this book"), unlike the introductory recitative spoken as part of a play (often by a character specifically identified as Prologue). Nonetheless, in addition to the clear intent to direct the remarks to a reader rather than a spectator, this prologue is characterized by the absence of any allusion to the fact that these works are to be acted. To be sure, reference is made to tragedies and to theatrical works. We search in vain, however, for any commentary by the dramatist which might aid us in understanding the dramatic content. Our observation should not be seen in a pejorative light. What emerges from this short prologue, significantly composed during the apogee of the Lopean *comedia* (as Virués's parenthetical comment confirms), is a concern for a theoretical justification rather than any renewed interest in the dramatic content of the plays which were composed some two decades earlier. Of the five dramas, only *Dido* is singled out as conforming to Classical principles. Froldi, as we noted, has suggested this emphasis as indicative of how atypical *Dido* appeared to Virués himself. We may, of course, accept the converse as well, namely, that Virués wished to show, in the early seventeenth century, how even in his youth the majority of his plays revealed a balance between Classical and contemporary dramatic theory. This is all the more likely in view of Virués's declaration that the other four plays *bring together* the best of "ancient art and modern custom." Accordingly, it is Virués himself who asks us to see the pivotal nature of his collection of dramatic works.

We should point out as well that the final reference to the reader in this prologue constitutes the conventional *captatio benevolentiae* or appeal to the good will of the reader. It is noteworthy that this final salute to the reader is included in a sentence which once more presents the Horatian pleasure-and-profit precept as well as a reminder that the author had also adhered to similar principles in his *Monserrate*. In summary, this prologue attempts to inform the reader of the nature of the artistic concerns which guided the author, rather than serve as an introduction to what Milton might have called "the matter of my song."[16]

III *The Prologue and Epilogue to* Cassandra

In the prologue just discussed, Virués does make one reference to the content of the plays when he mentions the "heroic and serious moral examples" which are set forth in them. The prologue to *Cruel Cassandra* also speaks of examples, and in much greater detail. We are warned that in *Cassandra* we shall find "examples of virtue, although perhaps shown by its opposite, vice" (p. 59). (I have discussed elsewhere what I have called Virués's didacticism "by opposite example,")[17] It is this kind of declaration that makes a study of the prologues and epilogues rewarding. Virués's penchant for violence and perversity, though often ascribed to an exaggerated Senecan influence, not only assumes a purpose beyond that of depicting monstrosities for the sake of dramatizing evil; the presentation of horrific scenes reflects more than a conception of tragedy as inevitably associated with death; the conscious intent to represent virtue by the presentation of "its opposite, vice," further strengthens the arguments presented in our chapter three with respect to an intuitive anticipation of a theater of the absurd. Additional weight for such an interpretation is found in the epilogue to this play, spoken by *Tragedia:*

> let those who, seeing me, themselves amuse
> beware that 'tis the difference twixt the painted and the live,
> and so by what I painted here present, the live
> be understood to be excessively contrived.   (p. 91)

It is, of course, possible to see in these closing lines a defensive pose with respect to the dangers (for the author, not for the audience) involved in any attempt to identify the iniquities portrayed in the work of art with the perhaps all too obvious analogues in living personages. Such an interpretation would serve to explain the bewilderment expressed by nearly every commentator on this play with respect to its historical sources. The very imprecision in this regard may be linked to the author's concern that the allusion to current events may be too transparent. This would explain as well why the king, the prince and the princess in this play remain anonymous. The relationship among these matters is a plausible explanation of what otherwise might remain far more conjectural, and this in itself reflects the importance of Virués's prologues and epilogues. On the other hand, we need neither to reject nor to accept this evaluation in order to see in the epilogue a clear recognition by the poet of his own excesses, which is to say that he was conscious of the very matters for which he was subsequently faulted by so many critics. To the extent that he knowingly presented "examples of virtue ... by its opposite, vice" in a manner "excessively contrived," the arguments for an intuitive sense of a theater of the absurd may be seen as that much more valid.

The prologue to *Cassandra* provides yet another perspective:

> ...virtue is advisable in the youth, in the old it is honorable and delightful, useful to the poor; to the rich, rich adornment; glory to the happy, to the unhappy consolation, luster of the nobility, *and great nobility for those who by their blood don't have it,* and finally the greatest good there is on earth.   (p. 58)

The general concept of honor as dependent upon virtue is stated in the opening lines of this prologue, in which Virués cites Alexander the Great, Socrates, and Aristotle. The italicized portion of the passage cited here (the emphasis is mine) not only aids us in identifying Virués's position on the relationship of honor and virtue — generally speaking, we may associate him more with Cervantes than with Lope in this respect[18] — but provides further support for Hermenegildo's cited thesis with respect to any "impurities" of blood in the poet's ancestry. It is, of course, incautious to apply the passage in this prologue to problems raised by speculations concerning Virués's biography. Nonetheless, the poet's personal sensibilities with respect to the ability of virtue to compensate for any lack of nobility clearly apply to our appreciation of his works.

The *Cassandra* prologue is of further interest to us because it contains the nucleus of what, decades later, Virués would declare in the prologue to the 1609 edition of all the plays. The "examples of virtue ... shown by its opposite, vice" will be "accompanied by sweet taste" (the Horatian principle once more), and in this, continues the prologue, the play will be following the best of "ancient art and modern usage" (p. 59). We may infer from this that not only in retrospect but at the time of the composition of these plays in the 1580s Virués was conscious of the pivotal approach to his art.

IV *The Prologue and Epilogue to* Attila

The prologue to *Furious Attila* reflects Virués's continuing concern with the power of love. Referring us to the mythical birth of Cupid as son of Venus and Mars, the prologue attempts to explain Cupid's behavior as the result of a sensuous mother and militant father. The conventionalism of these verses is evident, as is the relationship between unbridled passion and the immorality which pervades Attila's court.[19] That we are to see the exemplary nature of iniquity, which is to say the perception of virtue through the presentation of vice and its resultant chaos, is made clear by the epilogue — once again spoken by *Tragedia* —as the pleasure and profit principle is reiterated: "besides pleasure and entertainment, / let everyone derive doctrine / with which to awaken in himself divine virtue" (p. 117).

V *The Prologue and Epilogue to* Semíramis

Although the prologue to *Great Semíramis* is the most revealing

The Prologues and Epilogues

of any of those written for a specific play to the extent that it provides an appreciation of Virués's art, the epilogue recited by *Tragedia* deserves a comment for its unique way of expressing what we have just remarked upon above. The entire epilogue is one octave, with its typical rhyme scheme of *abababcc*. The rhyme of the first six lines attracts attention because the assonantal rhyme is composed of the same two vowels in all six lines, the difference being that the three even lines have a consonant between the rhyming vowels (typical of Spanish versification), since it is assonance that determines the rhyme with no intervening consonant. To be specific, the final words of the three even lines are *mulicia, cudicia, milicia,* and the final words of the odd lines *cortesía, valentía, tiranía.* (The stress on the final words of both sets is on the same vowel, the semiconsonantal *i* of the diphthong not affecting the rhyme, hence both sets may be said to have the same assonantal rhyme.) The intervening consonant in the even lines serves to set them apart from the odd lines, and this causes us to notice another aspect of some interest. The alternation in the first four lines corresponds to an oscillation between virtuous and vicious qualities. Accordingly, in the first line *Tragedia* speaks of valor, goodness, and courtesy; in the third line she speaks of discretion, love, and bravery. In contrast, line two deals with deceit, evil, and malice; line four refers to passion, rancor, and covetousness. The fifth and sixth lines seem to reverse the pattern — line five continues the pejorative tone of the fourth line and speaks of vice, cruelty, and tyranny; line six lists government, peace, and soldiery — until we take yet another look and notice that this sixth line, while referring to good qualities, is not so much in opposition to the preceding evils as it is a moralizing piece of advice on how the vices are to be dominated: harmony governed by discipline. When we recall the perverse elements in the plot of *Semíramis* — on the personal or microcosmic level as well as on the universal plane — the epilogue becomes an enlightening compendium of the play's motifs. As for its purpose, the final couplet of *Tragedia's* remarks once more explains that it is of the matters just enumerated that the play gives examples. The alternating pattern of good and evil combined with the exemplary purpose may now be understood to reflect once more the Horatian duo of pleasure and profit as well as Virués's penchant for illustrating virtue by demonstrating vice.

It is in the prologue to *Semíramis* that we find the most direct statement by Virués about his dramatic art. If in his other prologues he either did not concern himself with novelty or limited himself to a concern for the fusion of ancient and modern customs, here in this prologue there emerges a decided desire to attract attention to what he considers original. We have already discussed one of these matters, namely, that it is in this prologue that Virués speaks of the novelty (*novedad*) of being the first play to be in three acts. This is by no means the only innovation that Virués wishes to draw to our attention. Unhesitatingly referring to a "new style which [this play] introduces," Virués informs us that each of the three acts takes place at a different time (p. 26). But this is no mere flouting of the Classical unity of time; nor is the subsequent declaration that each act occurs in a different city simply a defiance of the unity of place. The originality, maintains Virués, consists of each act's assuming the nature of a separate tragedy in its own right and in accordance with artistic precepts. Most observers have commented on this imaginative twist with respect to the unities, but little has been said of it other than that it reflects a desire to be original. This it assuredly does and, together with the parallel insistence by Virués on the novelty of the three-act format, reveals that in contrast with some other prologues we have read, here Virués does indeed manifest a desire to be recognized for originality.

There remains an intriguing aspect whose full development lies outside the scope of the present volume. Leaving to one side the theoretical questions of tragedy as a mode or genre, as well as the controversial interpretation of the three unities, there is in the structure of *Semíramis,* and notably so because of Virués's insistence upon it in the prologue, the basis for one of the attributes of many a *comedia* of the subsequent — and more famous — dramatists of the Spanish Golden Age. This was brought out in an exchange which took place at the 1977 congress of the Asociación Internacional de Hispanistas, held in Toronto. Following the delivery of a paper by A. J. Valbuena Briones on Calderón's *Origen, pérdida y restauración de la Virgen del Sagrario,* A. A. Parker rose to praise the presentation, pointing out that he was intrigued by the description of Calderón's use of three separate phases, rather than a connected span, for the development of the drama. Mentioning a number of plays by Lope de Vega and Tirso de Molina, Parker went on to say that it was his belief that this aspect of the Spanish *comedia* has not been studied.[20] This interesting exchange between two well-known scholars is mentioned here not as an irrelevant anecdote but because the points raised in that discussion bear directly upon Virués's declaration in the *Semíramis* prologue that this is the "new style" which he introduces in this play. Whether he is truly the first may ultimately be placed in doubt by subsequent research. What is important at this juncture is to bear in mind that, as in the case of the three-act format, Virués appears to believe himself to be the innovator, and if Lope de Vega was willing to give him credit for the one aspect, it may well be that, consciously or not, the "creator" of the Spanish *comedia* may have found inspiration for the other aspect in Virués as well.

Before moving on to the final section of this chapter, it should be noted that in the preceding paragraph lies the clearest explanation of why we have chosen "pivotal" to describe Virués, rather than some more conventional term like "precursor" or "forerunner." The chronology alone, of course, justifies these last terms, but as we have tried to show, the oscillating movement of Virués's approaches suggests the image of a pivot rather than a spot on a chronological scale. We have also avoided the image of the pendulum, for it is not our intention to suggest ambivalence — a posture we have attributed to his critics — but rather a central point of artistic concern around which the varying attitudes of ancient and modern, Italian and Spanish, revolved, Lest it be thought that this places Cristóbal de Virués in the unique position at the center of artistic developments, we must refer to our preface, in which we stressed Virués's position as typical of a host of kindred spirits. All of these together belong in this center from which would evolve the subsequently established principles of Spanish art (in all its forms) as embodied in the works of the giants in the decades to follow. In this respect, then, Virués, along with others in a period of experimentation, played a pivotal role as, for example, his mutation of the Classical and neo-Aristotelian interpretations of tragedy helped swing the theater toward a newer definition.

VI *The Prologue and Epilogue to* Marcela

The foregoing assessment must be kept in mind as we consider the prologue to the play which, as we have noted, most closely approaches the drama of Virués's successors. Sargent (p. 108) declares that in the prologue to *Marcela* Virués "addresses his public a bit defiantly, as though he were failing to receive the support he felt due him ..." Hermenegildo similarly refers to the "defiant tone in which the prologue is written" and goes on to suggest that it is a "probable testimony to Virués's failure before the public with his previous works...."[21] These observations deal with the prologue's references to the "vain wind of the masses" (*el vano viento del vulgo*) and the compensatory consolation he expects from the learned who will be in his favor (p. 119). Yet, as both Sargent and Hermenegildo are quick to point out, these sardonic comments contrast sharply with the popular quality of the play they introduce. We should also bear in mind that ridiculing in a prologue is another commonplace, and that sarcastic comments about the masses are not absent in the writings of Lope de Vega. We have no evidence that prevents an antithetical interpretation, namely, that precisely because this prologue introduces the play most in accord with the tastes of the masses, the references to the learned (*sabios*) may in fact be the ironic statement of a writer who has seen the anachronism of the adherence to outmoded precepts.

The epilogue, again recited by *Tragedia,* does not make sarcastic references to the audience, addressing the latter as "most high listeners," again a commonplace of no extraordinary significance. Of interest, however, is a line which could readily serve as a definition of theater, as *Tragedia* refers to "the truth which in me you note pretended" (p. 145). This is not only an interesting variation of the Aristotelian concept of the poetic truth, but leaves in the minds of the departing audience a typically baroque enigma: have we just witnessed a universal truth portrayed in a fictive manner, or have we seen a make-believe truth? That we may progress from a medieval through a renaissance and now to a baroque interpretation of Virués's works is the clearest expression of the essence of this poet's contribution to Spanish literature.

Notes and References

Preface

1. During much of this period Virués lived in Italy, important for its influence upon his literary work. We possess no documentation other than his own poetry with its many allusions, from which Sargent and Münch have derived a biographical sketch of Virués in Italy. I refer the reader to these works (identified below) rather than attempt a new "reading between the lines."

Chapter One

1. Fernand Braudel, *The Mediterranean and the Mediterranean World in the Age of Philip II* (New York: Harper & Row, 1973), II, 1088.

2. J. H. Elliott, *Imperial Spain: 1469-1716* (New York: Mentor Books, 1966), p. 238.

3. See J. H. Elliott, *Europe Divided: 1559-1598* (New York: Harper & Row, 1968), p. 198, who finds it "hard to believe that the eventual outcome in the Mediterranean would have been very different [even if Spain had been willing or able to follow up Lepanto with energy], while Spain's capacity for war in Northern Europe would have been profoundly affected.... Already, within a year or two of Lepanto, the focus of conflict was beginning to shift — from the struggle between non-Christian East and Christian West, to that between Catholic South and Protestant North." Cf. Cecilia V. Sargent, *The Dramatic Works of Cristóbal de Virués* (New York: Instituto de las Españas, 1930), pp. 34-36: "... in spite of the splendid victory won at such cost at Tunis, 1573, the following year it soon fell again into the hands of the Turks, who presently held all Cyprus, as though Lepanto had never been."

4. *Don Quixote de la Mancha*, I, 6. Cited from the translation by Samuel Putnam (New York: Viking, 1949). Ercilla's *Araucana* is well known for its depiction of the Spanish campaign to conquer the Araucanian Indians of Chile and is especially noted for its description of the courage of the Indians. Less familiar is Juan Rufo's *Austriada* (1584), revolving around the exploits of Don John of Austria. It concludes with the battle of Lepanto and is preceded by several preliminary poems, including a sonnet by Cervantes. A dissertation currently in preparation promises to provide us with a critical edition of Rufo's poem. The editor is Magdalena

Mora, according to *Hispania,* 59 (1976), 286.

6. Sargent ventures no guess about the precise date of the poet's birth. Francisco Martí Grajales, in his *Ensayo de un diccionario biográfico y bibliográfico de los poetas ... de Valencia hasta el año 1700* (Madrid: RABM, 1927), p. 474, accepts 1550 as the year of birth, as do Francisco Ruiz Ramón, *Historia del teatro español* (Madrid: Alianza, 1971), I, 110, and Alfredo Hermenegildo, *La tragedia del renacimiento español* (Barcelona: Planeta, 1973), p. 208. Among other authorities to whom I shall refer on subsequent matters, the following do not discuss the question of the birthdate: Henri Mérimée, *L'Art dramatique à Valencia* (Toulouse: Privat, 1913); J. P. Wickersham Crawford, *Spanish Drama Before Lope de Vega* (1937; rpt. Philadelphia: Univ. of Pennsylvania Press, 1967); Eduardo Juliá Martínez, ed., *Poetas dramáticos valencianos,* 2 vols. (Madrid: Real Academia Española, 1929); Rinaldo Froldi, *Lope de Vega y la formación de la Comedia* (Salamanca: Anaya, 1968).

7. Among them: Leandro Fernández de Moratín, in his *Catálogo histórico y crítico de piezas dramáticas anteriores a Lope de Vega,* in *Biblioteca de Autores Españoles,* 2 (Madrid: Rivadeneyra, 1846); apparently Crawford (*Spanish Drama...*, p. 182), who refers to 1609 as "the close of his life"; Angel Valbuena Prat, *Historia de la literatura española* (Barcelona: Gili, 1964), II, 782; Otis H. Green, *Spain and the Western Tradition* (Madison: Univ. of Wisconsin Press, 1965) III, 113; Ruiz Ramón, *op. cit.,* I, 110; and Alva V. Ebersole, ed., *Selección de comedias del Siglo de Oro español* (Madrid: Castalia, 1973), p. 75. (Ebersole's source is the conjecture of several critics, for which he credits Sargent, but Sargent herself as we shall see, is inclined to accept a much later date despite what she acknowledges to be the general opinion.)

8. The reference is to a Pedro de Aguilar. There is every reason to agree with Sargent's reasoning (p. 3) that Gaspar de Aguilar, the Valencian dramatist (1561-1623), is the poet Cervantes had in mind. Moreover, in his voluminous *Diccionario biográfico y bibliográfico...*, Martí Grajales lists three Aguilars, but none with the given name of Pedro. The context of Cervantes's lines, in which he refers to these poets as a *junta famosa de las que Turia en sus riberas cría* (famous group of the sort Turia raises by its banks), leaves no doubt that he is referring to poets of Valencia, the city of the river Turia. On the other hand, it should be recalled that in *Don Quixote,* I, 39, Cervantes also refers to a Pedro de Aguilar, poet of Andalusia.

9. The fourth member of the group, Luis Ferrer de Cardona, was born in 1568 and died in 1641. (The reference to Julio Cejador y Frauca is to his *Historia de la lengua y literatura castellana,* cited by Sargent, pp. 2-3.)

10. Sargent, p. 3. *Criar* means "to bring up" or "raise" in the sense of bringing up one's children. See note 8 above.

11. Miguel de Cervantes, *La Galatea,* book VI ("Canto de Calíope").

12. Lope de Vega, *El laurel de Apolo,* silva IV.

Notes and References

13. Valencia is still today antonomastically referred to as the "city of the Turia."

14. See Vicente Ximeno, *Escritores del reyno de Valencia,* I (Valencia: Dolz, 1747), 96. The humanist ideal implanted in our poet's memory may be noted in an interesting allusion to John Hus in canto 14 of the *Monserrate,* in which Garín's attitude while facing death at the hands of cannibals is depicted as the "true portrait" of Hus.

15. Martí Grajales, p. 475.

16. I have discussed the *Academia de los Nocturnos* and related literary societies in *The Valencian Dramatists of Spain's Golden Age* (Boston: Twayne, 1976), pp. 13-15. See also José Sánchez, *Academias literarias del Siglo de Oro español* (Madrid: Gredos, 1961) and Willard F. King, *Prosa novelística y academias literarias en el siglo XVII* (Madrid: Real Academia Española, 1963).

17. Ximeno, I, 214, lists these and three others. However, Francisco Martí Grajales, ed., *Cancionero de la Academia de los Nocturnos de Valencia,* 4 vols. (Valencia: Imprenta de F. Vives Mora, 1905-12), does not include these among the many others (primarily of a religious nature) by Jerónimo which may be found in the *Cancionero.*

18. *Selección de comedias...,* p. 75.

19. *Poetas dramáticos valencianos,* I, xlvi. Virués's residence in Italy, as well as the Italian influence evident in some of his works as noted by a number of commentators, raises speculation concerning possible attendance at, if not membership in, some of the prominent academies of that nation. See, for example, the opening statement by R. S. Samuels, "Benedetto Varchi ... and the Origins of the Italian Academic Movement," *Renaissance Quarterly,* 29 (1976), 599: "The sixteenth-century Italian academies, in the judgment of modern scholars, played a role in the intellectual life of their time and had an impact on the culture of their age to an extent not yet fully assessed."

20. See the discussion later in this chapter with respect to the chronology of Virués's works.

21. *Historia del Monserrate del Capitán Cristóbal de Virués,* ed. Cayetano Rosell, *Biblioteca de Autores Españoles,* 17 (1849; rpt. Madrid: Atlas, 1945), 515. Subsequent references to the *Monserrate* will come from this edition and will be cited in the text.

22. Cited from Sargent, p. 11. I have modernized the spelling, as I shall do in all Spanish quotations from Virués's works, unless the original is required for rhyme or rhythm. In this I am not following Virués's own wishes, which I would do were I preparing a critical edition. See Sargent, pp. 156-58, and Juliá, I, xlix. Virués's own explanation is found in the prologue to the *Monserrate.*

23. If we take him literally, Virués was among the injured: "three thousand of us Christians were we wounded." His count appears to have been conservative; most historians estimate 8,000 killed and between 15,000

and 20,000 wounded on the Christian side.

24. The initial sound of the four-times-stated *quien,* as well as of *cual,* corresponds to our English *k.*

25. All references to Virués's five dramas are taken from vol. I of the edition by Juliá Martínez cited in note 6, and will be indicated in the text. Yet another example, written in 1605 at the probable age of fifty-five, is found in a poem which I quote only in Spanish, my purpose being not to analyze its content (the subject is the disillusionment with the military life), but to demonstrate how consistently over the years Virués would depict warfare with the same consonantal alliteration:

> *Quien nos llama caballos desbocados,*
> *quien lobos carniceros y atrevidos,*
> *quien toros acosados y afligidos,*
> *quien leones sangrientos y aquejados.* (Sargent, p. 35)

26. The original Spanish is found in Sargent, p. 13.

27. See Elliott, *Europe Divided,* pp. 195-96: "Don John, the bastard son of an emperor, spent much of his brief and poignant life scheming for a crown, and he may for a moment have toyed with the idea of becoming king of Tunis. But in the end he left the city with a Spanish garrison and a native governor, together with the unsolved problem of how to defend itself in the probable event of a Turkish counter-attack."

28. Melveena McKendrick, *Woman and Society in the Spanish Drama of the Golden Age: A Study of the "Mujer Varonil"* (London: Cambridge Univ. Press, 1974), pp. 61-62.

29. J. Hurtado and A. González Palencia, *Historia de la literatura española* (Madrid: RABM, 1925), p. 386.

30. My own copy of the book was given to me by its first owner, who had received it as a gift upon completing his doctor of philosophy examinations at Harvard in 1939. It is inscribed by a member of that distinguished faculty: "To ———, for his last and best exam. Sincere congratulations." My point is not to ridicule, but rather to underscore that the judgments in that book were standard fare in the *best* curricula.

31. Leandro Fernández de Moratín, "Discurso sobre los orígenes del teatro español," *Biblioteca de Autores Españoles,* 2 (1830; rpt. Madrid: Atlas, 1944), 248-70.

32. *Lope de Vega y la formación de la Comedia,* pp. 111-12.

33. *La tragedia en el renacimiento español,* p. 208, a repetition of his misquote of a dozen years earlier in his *Los trágicos españoles del siglo XVI* (Madrid: Fundación Universitaria Española, 1961), p. 215. See Sargent, p. 14.

34. Mérimée, *L'Art dramatique à Valencia,* p. 331; Crawford, *Spanish Drama Before Lope de Vega,* p. 182; Ruiz Ramón, *Historia del teatro español,* I, 115.

Notes and References

35. Sargent, p. 144.
36. See the chapter on *Marcela* in the present book.
37. Froldi, p. 112.
38. Cayetano Rosell, in his introduction and catalogue of epic poems, *Biblioteca de Autores Españoles,* 29 (1849; rpt. Madrid: Atlas, 1948), xxvii. The Ximeno work is the same one referred to in note 14 above. The reference to Nicolás Antonio is to the latter's *Bibliotheca Hispana Nova* (Madrid, 1783). The same insistence is found preceding Rosell's edition of the *Monserrate,* p. 503. In a careful analysis of Virués's poetry, Münch similarly has occasion to insist on 1588, criticizing Ximeno for the 1587 date, but giving no reason. See E. F. J. von Münch-Bellinghausen, "Virués Leben und Werke," *Jahrbuch für romanische und englische Literatur,* II (1860), 151.
39. *Poetas dramáticos valencianos,* I, xlvii.
40. *L'Art dramatique à Valencia,* p. 681: "L'impression de l'ouvrage était achevée le 11 décembre 1587."
41. Sargent, p. 18. The reference is to Cristóbal Pérez Pastor, *Bibliografía madrileña* (Madrid, 1891-97).
42. Sargent, p. 18.
43. *Diccionario,* p. 477: "Sólo se diferencia de la anterior en la fecha de la portada."
44. Frank Pierce, *La poesía épica del Siglo de Oro* (Madrid: Gredos, 1968), p. 336. In the text of his book, Pierce simply indicates the date of the *Monserrate* as 1587, without any explanation, the clarification being found quite logically in the bibliography where the details just mentioned are described. In an earlier work, *The Heroic Poem of the Spanish Golden Age* (New York: Oxford Univ. Press, 1947), Pierce dates the *Monserrate* as 1588. The more recent study reflects Pierce's subsequent research.
45. In the oft-quoted prologue to his *Ocho comedias y ocho entremeses* (Eight *Comedias* and Eight Interludes), Cervantes presents a concise summary of the Spanish theater of the sixteenth century up to the "rise of that monster of nature, the great Lope de Vega and his comic monarchy." (The word *comedia,* which I shall use repeatedly throughout this book, is not strictly synonymous with our English word "comedy" and should be considered as a generic term for that sort of drama which Lope de Vega helped make into a national genre, although he did not create it, as many textbooks still suggest.)
46. Cited from the translation by William T. Brewster, in *Papers on Playmaking,* ed. Brander Matthews (New York: Hill and Wang, 1957), p. 16. I have substituted *comedia* for Brewster's "comedy" for the reason given in the preceding note.
47. Cited by Brewster, p. 279.
48. *Ibid.*
49. *Spanish Drama Before Lope de Vega,* p. 183. Virués makes a more surprising claim in some verses cited by Münch, "Virués Leben und

Werke," p. 162:

> Of ancient and grave true history
> I formed a new true poem,
> Following with Virgil and with Homer
> The heroic art in its most polished form.
> If I didn't get as far as I would like
> Along that high celestial path,
> Excuse me, for in Spain I was the first
> Who undertook along that road to pass.

Once more, the value in these lines does not lie in their inaccurate account of who was first to undertake the writing of heroic poetry in Spain. They do tell us something of our poet's need to proclaim originality while admitting he could not equal the efforts of the Greek and Roman poets. See our chapter 5.

50. Ximeno, p. 247. The reference is to Vich's *Breve discurso en favor de las comedias*, 1650. Martí Grajales, *Diccionario*, p. 466, describes a *Breue discurso* by Vich and quotes Vich as saying that the *comedia* was not yet a hundred years old, that it had been of four acts until "our Captain Artieda was the first to put it in three; and later, in larger shoes [*mayores chapines*] Lope de Vega and Miguel Sánchez in Castile, Gaspar Aguilar and the Canon Tárrega in Valencia." (Note the similarity of the metaphors employed by Vich and Lope, describing the *comedia* as a child with feet or shoes.)

51. In the prologue cited in note 45 above.

52. Hermenegildo, *La tragedia...*, p. 586, shares the opinion of Salvá, *Catálogo de la biblioteca de Salvá* (Valencia, 1872) that there was an earlier edition, but this remains unconfirmed.

53. The *New Art* was first published in 1609, although a number of scholars have postulated an earlier edition. Juana de José Prades, in her edition (Madrid: C.S.I.C., 1971), p. 17, dates the actual composition of the poem 1605-1608. We cannot, of course, rule out Lope's having seen a manuscript, but this would be pure conjecture. There is room for further conjecture which casts Lope in a somewhat different light as the result of what may be a greater familiarity with Virués's works than we are suggesting here. This does not alter our understanding of the works of Virués, but it enhances our comprehension of Lope de Vega's self image. See John G. Weiger, "Lope's Role in the Lope de Vega Myth," *Hispania*, forthcoming. See also Joseph G. Fucilla, "Lope and Calderón's *La hija del aire*," *Bulletin of the Comediantes*, 27 (1975), 90-91.

54. Juana de José Prades, p. 3n.

55. *Ibid.*, p. 148. Lope's first visit to Valencia occurred in 1588; the second in 1599. It is unlikely that Virués was in Valencia during the years 1591-94, the period of activity of the *Academia de los Nocturnos* in which he did not participate. The 1599 visit of Lope is the more likely one to pos-

tulate a friendship between the two, and the date is also closer to the 1604 publication of the *Rimas*.

56. A[lfred] Morel-Fatio, "*L'Arte nuevo de hazer comedias en este tiempo,* de Lope de Vega," *Bulletin Hispanique,* 3 (1901), 369.

57. José Prades, *op. cit.,* p. 148.

58. In my translation of these lines in *The Valencian Dramatists of Spain's Golden Age,* p. 31, I translated *los mejores principios que tuvieron* as "the best principles they owned." I now render this line as "the best beginnings they did behold." *Principios* may mean either "principles" or "beginnings." Atkinson (see note 60 below) evidently read it as "principles" as well, although he avoids a translation (because of the ambiguity?) but nonetheless reflects this meaning in the context of his quotation: "Lope derived his *mejores principios,* his deepest and most fruitful inspiration, from Virués" (p. 115). I would argue now that the principles of the comic muses are not being credited to Virués (does a poet inspire the muses?), but rather that the muses saw their best beginnings (that is, the comedic genre bore the fruit of the muses) in the plays of Virués.

59. José Prades, *op. cit.,* p. 148. The quotation is used to support, not establish, her contention.

60. William C. Atkinson, "Séneca, Virués, Lope de Vega," in *Homenatge a Antoni Rubió i Lluch* (Barcelona: Estudis Universitaris Catalans, 1936), I, 115.

61. Justo Pastor Fuster, *Biblioteca valenciana de los escritores que florecieron hasta nuestros días* (Valencia: José Ximeno, 1827), p. 205.

62. As we have noted, the date of the *Laurel de Apolo* is 1630. At about the same time (1631), according to Morley and Bruerton's chronology of Lope's *comedias* (see the bibliography) Lope composed *El castigo sin venganza.* C. A. Jones cites Lope's description of the work as a *tragedia* written "in the Spanish manner, and not in the manner of Greek antiquity and Latin severity...." Jones then observes: "It is true that Lope may have been hitting at the Valencian tragedians and at other traditionalists like Cervantes (as far as drama was concerned) rather than at the ancients; but his 'Spanish style' could hardly be said to diverge from that of his predecessors and contemporaries in the direction of neo-Aristotelianism." See C. A. Jones, "Tragedy in the Spanish Golden Age," in *The Drama of the Renaissance: Essays for Leicester Bradner,* ed. Elmer M. Blistein (Providence: Brown Univ. Press, 1970), pp. 103–104. If it is indeed true that in 1631 Lope "may have been hitting at the Valencian tragedians," then the 1630 eulogy for Virués needs to be seen in yet another light.

63. Brewster translation, p. 15.

Chapter Two

1. The total perimeter is approximately sixteen miles, divided roughly

into lengths of six miles and a width of nearly four miles.

2. Throughout the present book a distinction will be maintained between the poem, *Monserrate*, and the place, Montserrat.

3. José María Girabal, *Legends of Montserrat,* trans. Joseph McKee (Barcelona: Editorial Balmes, 1974), n. pag.

4. The booklet described in the preceding note presents a concise, if somewhat elementary, summary of the legends associated with the mountain. The most complete historical account of Montserrat is found in Anselm M. Albareda, *Historia de Montserrat*, rev. ed. by Josep Massot i Muntaner (Barcelona: Abadia de Montserrat, 1974).

5. George Ticknor, *History of Spanish Literature* (New York: Gordian Press, 1965), II, 559.

6. Longinus, *On the Sublime,* 19:2, trans. T. S. Dorsch (Harmondsworth: Penguin, 1965).

7. See Demetrius, *On Style,* 5:268.

8. Longinus, *op. cit.,* 20:3.

9. See Gilbert Highet, *The Classical Tradition: Greek and Roman Influences on Western Literature* (London: Oxford Univ. Press, 1957), pp. 144-61, 601-11.

10. Thomas Bulfinch, *The Age of Fable,* ed. E. E. Hale (Boston: Tilton, 1881), p. 455. Cf. the second strophe of Tasso's *Jerusalem Delivered,* trans. [1600] Edward Fairfax (New York: Capricorn, 1963):

> O heavenly muse, that not with fading bays
> Deckest thy brow by th' Heliconian spring,
> But sittest, crown'd with stars' immortal rays,
> In heaven where legions of bright angels sing,
> Inspire life in my wit, my thoughts upraise,
> My verse ennoble, and forgive the thing,
> If fictions light I mix with truth divine,
> And fill these lines with others' praise than thine.

Tasso's work, though written earlier, was not published until 1581. Virués presumably was familiar with the original Italian, but it is of interest to note that the first Spanish translation was not published until 1587, the year of the *Monserrate's* publication.

11. Highet, The Classical Tradition, p. 608, recalls that it has been suggested that Tasso had in mind the Virgin Mary. Interestingly, it is in canto 18 of the *Monserrate* — a canto reserved for the miraculous appearance of the image of the Virgin and Child on Montserrat — that Virués makes a similar identification. In fact, it is a progressively stronger association: the first strophe simply invokes the muse ("Oh muse!"); the second strophe calls upon the "divine muse"; the third strophe is a direct appeal to the Virgin:

> You, most holy Queen of the world,

> Of its great Redeemer mother pious;
> You, divine Empress of heaven,
> Of the Holy Spirit beloved spouse;
> You, aid and light, guide and consolation
> Of this unworthy soul that dares to call you thus;
> You I invoke, you my Lady mine,
> I ask for consolation, light, comforting guide.

Of no small consideration is the form of address here: the Spanish *vos,* as compared with the *tú* when addressing the muse in the initial canto. These forms were undergoing transition during the period in question, but a helpful distinction is provided by Gerald E. Wade in his edition of Tirso de Molina's *El burlador de Sevilla* (New York: Scribner's, 1969), p. 175: "It should be observed that during the Golden Age the *tú* was used, as now, for intimate conversation, but it was also employed by an inferior to a superior (somewhat as in English we use *Thou* to the deity).... The *vos* form was the normal address beweeen equals among the gentility...."

12. Among the several excellent works on the subject, C. S. Lewis's *Allegory of Love* not only provides a careful examination but shows as well, particularly in the chapter titled "Allegory," the multifarious interpretations of the term and its confusion with symbolism.

13. Rhodes Dunlap, "The Allegorical Interpretation of Renaissance Literature," *PMLA,* 82 (1967), 39.

14. Aristotle, *Poetics,* 9:1-5, trans. Gerald F. Else (Ann Arbor: Univ. of Michigan Press, 1970), pp. 32-33.

15. Cf. Charles S. Singleton's observation on the opening line of Dante's *Divine Comedy:* "The importance of 'nostra' is not to be overlooked. This is 'our' life's journey, and we are necessarily involved in it. Thus, in its first adjective, the poem is open to the possibility of allegory." Cited from vol. I, part 2 ("Commentary") to Singleton's edition of the *Divine Comedy: Inferno* (Princeton: Princeton Univ. Press, 1970), pp. 3-4.

16. Tartarus is the underworld of Classical mythology, as Acheron, Cocytus, Phlegethon, and Lethe are the rivers of woe, lamentation, fire, and oblivion, respectively. See Virgil's *Aeneid,* VI, 656-59. See also Milton's *Paradise Lost,* II, 578-83. A concise definition may be found in Edith Hamilton, *Mythology* (New York: New American Library, 1969), p. 39. For a biblical identification of the Devil and Satan, particularly with respect to the "great and fearful battle" to which the Satan of Virués's poem alludes, see Revelation 20:1-10.

17. For example, we could indulge in the symbolic interpretation of the nine days which the girl — according to Satan's instructions — must spend in Garín's cave. An investigation of the symbolism of the number nine would not be without profit. As we shall see, however, the significance of the stay with Garín as a novena is more relevant to the poem as a whole. (That a novena itself is readily interpreted through numerical symbolism is

not as meaningful here as is the simple irony of the devil's choice of a Catholic devotional concept.)

18. J.E. Cirlot, *A Dictionary of Symbols* (New York: Philosophical Library, 1962), pp. 221-22.

19. For a true parody of the Trinity, see Dante's description of the three faces of the devil in the final canto of the *Inferno*. Virués has his Satan summon a host of his ministers, which he describes as an "immense squadron of wild people" and from among whom he selects the cruelest and most furious to play the roles of the two subalterns in our poem.

20. The Spanish reads *triones*, a latinism which itself is an abbreviation of the Latin *septentriones* (in turn derived from *septem triones* or "seven plough-oxen"), signifying the seven stars ("Big Dipper") of the constellation *Ursa Major* or Great Bear. The significance here is "above the stars," i.e., heaven, specifically above the Great and Small Bears, constellations (in the Northern Hemisphere) which never sink below the horizon. There is some irony in Satan's identification of this constellation as a reference point for the heights of heaven, inasmuch as the mythological origin of the bear constellations derives from the goddess Hera's jealousy of Callisto. See Bulfinch, pp. 41-42.

21. Cf. Bacon, "Of Envy": "It is also the vilest affection, and the most depraved; for which cause it is the proper attribute of the devil, who is called, *the envious man, that soweth tares amongst the wheat by night*" (italics in the original). See *The Essays or Counsels, Civil and Moral, of Francis [Bacon]* (Mount Vernon, N.Y.: Peter Pauper Press, n.d.), p. 40.

22. My reference to a hierarchy is based primarily on moral attributes (saints are superior to ordinary men; men are superior to devils) and to some extent on the common acceptance of the figurative location (the heights of heaven and the depths of hell). For a different orientation (in contrast with the foregoing point of view of increasing goodness as the criterion for ascending the scale), see C. S. Lewis, *The Discarded Image* (London: Cambridge Univ. Press, 1967), pp. 40-41: Plato, says Lewis, draws a clear distinction between "divine" and "daemoniac" which was to be influential for centuries. "Daemons are ... creatures of a middle nature between gods and men — like Milton's 'Middle spirits... Betwixt the angelical and human kind' [*Paradise Lost*, III, 461].... The daemons have bodies of a finer consistency than clouds, which are not normally visible to us. It is because they have bodies that [Apuleius] calls them animals: obviously he does not mean that they are beasts. They are rational (aerial) animals, as we are rational (terrestrial) animals, and the gods proper are rational (aetherial) animals." Compare *Paradise Lost*, III, 418-22:

> Meanwhile upon the firm opacous Globe
> Of this round World, whose first convex divides
> The luminous inferior Orbs, enclos'd

> From Chaos and th' inroad of Darkness old,
> Satan alighted walks....

In the two finest analyses of the concept of the chain of being, no place is reserved for Satan. See A. O. Lovejoy, *The Great Chain of Being* (Cambridge, Mass.: Harvard Univ. Press, 1963), and E. M. W. Tillyard, *The Elizabethan World Picture* (New York: Random House, n.d.). The work which is generally acknowledged to provide the best poetic statement of the concept, Pope's *Essay on Man,* stresses the proper order of the various links in the "vast chain of being," but similarly makes no reference to the place held for fallen angels, specifically the one whose fall was the result of an attempted reordering of the harmonious structure. Somewhat more akin to my own perspective is Dante's description of Beelzebub's residence in the center to which "he fell down from Heaven." See *Inferno,* canto 34. The association of the devil with a serpent also supports his position in a lower order.

23. Cited by Theodore Spencer, *Shakespeare and the Nature of Man* (New York: Macmillan, 1966), pp. 11-12.

24. According to at least one version of the legend, the girl's name was Riquilda (a hispanicized form of the Gothic Richilda or Richilde). See Cayetano Cornet y Mas, *Tres Días en Montserrat* (Barcelona: Plus Ultra, 1858), p. 24. With respect to the significance of the girl's beauty, consider the statement by Dostoevsky in *The Brothers Karamazov:* "Beauty is the battlefield where God and the devil contend with one another for the heart of man."

25. Genesis 3:8-9. There is less irony in the similar questions put to Cain (Genesis 4:9-10), in which it is easier for us to apprehend the meaning as being not a direct question but a rhetorical means of underscoring the answer which God knows as well as Adam or Cain. Cf. the words of the god Wotan in Act III of Wagner's *Die Walküre,* following Brünnhilde's transgression of the previous act: *Wo ist Brünnhilde? Wo die Verbrecherin? Wagt ihr, die Böse vor mir zu bergen?* ("Where is Brünnhilde? Where the transgressor? Dare you Valkyries to hide the evil woman from me?").

26. Session V, June 1546. Cited from *Documents of the Christian Church,* ed. Henry Bettenson (New York: Oxford Univ. Press, 1947), p. 368. Cf. Romans 5:12.

27. *Documents of the Christian Church,* p. 369 (session VI, January 1547).

28. *Ibid.,* p. 371 (session XIV, November 1551).

29. *Ibid.*

30. *La poesía épica del Siglo de Oro,* p. 291.

31. The Spanish word *peregrino* not only means "alien" or "strange," but is the customary word for "pilgrim."

32. The reference is to Philip II.

33. Horace, *On the Art of Poetry,* trans. T.S. Dorsch (Harmondsworth: Penguin, 1965), p. 84. Along with Aristotle, Horace is cited by Virués in the opening sentence of the prologue to the *Monserrate.*

34. The cockleshell or *venera* has the added significance of being an insignia worn by pilgrims who had visited the shrine of Santiago de Compostela. The suggestion would seem to be that even as an infant, Juan Garín had arrived as a pilgrim. On the allegorical level, it is easily perceived as man's voyage through life. (The island described by Virués appears to be pure invention. No island — and precious little water — is to be found at the mouth of the Llobregat today. Efforts to substantiate the island's earlier existence have proved fruitless on my part.)

35. Singleton, *op. cit.,* vol. I, part 2, p. 3. Singleton also quotes a Latin version of Isaiah 38:10, *Ego dixi: In dimidio dierum meorum vadam ad portas inferi* ("I said: In the midst of my days I shall go to the gates of hell").

36. Joseph Campbell, *The Hero with a Thousand Faces* (Princeton: Princeton Univ. Press, 1968), p. 322. Even a more historical description of Gregory's life and philosophy remains in accord with Garín's behavior and attitudes. For a concise account, see Will Durant, *The Age of Faith* (New York: Simon and Schuster, 1950), pp. 519-24.

37. Oscar Mandel, *A Definition of Tragedy* (New York: New York Univ. Press, 1961), pp. 103-104. We need not, for our present purpose, split hairs over the distinction between tragedy and epic which, in my opinion, are not different genres as much as they are different modes of artistic representation. What is to the point here is that, whatever the nature of the *Monserrate,* the monk Garín has been endowed with attributes of the hero.

38. Erich Auerbach, *Mimesis* (Princeton: Princeton Univ. Press, 1968), p. 5. Consider the elucidating attempt of C. S. Lewis to account for the phenomenon of the apparent digression: "Another explanation might be based in Rhetoric. Rhetoric recommended *morae* — delays or padding. Does all this science and 'story' come in simply *longius ut sit opus,* 'that the work may be longer'? But this perhaps overlooks the fact that Rhetoric explains the formal, not the material, characteristic. That is, it may tell you to digress; not what to put into your digressions.... [If the] digressions are filled with a certain sort of matter, this must be because writers and their audience liked it. Digression need not deal with the large, permanent features of the universe unless you want. The long-tailed similes in Homer ... usually do not.... The lost art of Pageant loved to re-state similar themes. And it has lately been shown that many Renaissance pictures which were once thought purely fanciful are loaded, and almost overloaded, with philosophy.... The simplest explanation is, I believe, the true one. Poets and other artists depicted these things because their minds loved to dwell on them.... Every particular fact and story became more interesting and more pleasurable if, by being properly fitted in, it

carried one's mind back to the [universal] Model as a whole" (*The Discarded Image*, pp. 200-203).

A correspondence between this narrative technique and the *in medias res* structure of the plot is found in Jacques Amyot's prologue to his translation of Heliodorus's *Ethiopian History* (French version, 1547; Spanish translation, 1554): "And certainly the disposition is extraordinary, because [Heliodorus] begins in the middle of the history, *just as heroic poets do;* and this immediately causes the readers to marvel and arouses in them the passionate desire to hear and understand the beginning; and moreover the author maintains their attention through the ingenious relating of his story, for they do not understand what they have read at the beginning of the first book until they see the end of the fifth; and when they have arrived at that point, they find themselves even more eager to see the end than they have been to see the beginning." (Cited from Alban K. Forcione, *Cervantes, Aristotle, and the "Persiles"* [Princeton: Princeton Univ. Press, 1970], p. 61. The italics are those of Forcione. See also pp. 71-76 for further elaboration.)

39. Forcione, p. 73. The translation and the italics in both the translation and the commentary are by Forcione.

40. There is no intent in the use of the word "create" to imply the origin of a genre. See, however, Angel Valbuena Prat, *Historia de la literatura española* (Barcelona: Gili, 1964), II, 275: "The last years of that generation [of the reign of Philip II], were showing the way. Luis Barahona de Soto in 1586 defined the epic style in imitation of Ariosto.... On the other hand, one year later [Valbuena evidently accepted the 1587 publication date] with less sonority and poetic affectation, the dramatist Virués defined the poem of saints as it would develop at the dawn of the seventeenth century, in his entangled and prosaic *Monserrate*...."

41. *De tejas arriba* (literally "from the roof tiles on up") and *de tejas abajo* ("from the roof tiles on down") are defined by the Royal Spanish Academy as, respectively, "of a supernatural order, dependent upon God's will," and "of a normal order, not dependent upon supernatural causes."

42. Otis H. Green, *Spain and the Western Tradition*, II (Madison: Univ. of Wisconsin Press, 1964), 180.

43. *Ibid.*, p. 292.

44. *Ibid.*, p. 312. Part of this quotation is credited by Green to an unpublished doctoral dissertation by Helen L. Sears. See also Green's "Sobre las dos Fortunas: de tejas arriba y de tejas abajo," in *Studia Philologica: Homenaje a Dámaso Alonso*, II (Madrid: Gredos, 1961), 143-54.

45. Without resorting to capitalization, we shall understand by "providence" the divine order and by "fortune" the vicissitudes of life.

46. That this aspect of Garin's life is providential can be seen by comparison with Green's reference to Pedro Simón Abril's *Filosofía natural* (ca. 1589): "The ancients, [Simón Abril] says, philosophized erroneously

about Fortune, as they did about other matters having to do with religion. In philosophy, he explains, Chance or Fortune is the rare coming together of two causes possessing entire independence of each other. For a man to walk along a road is a voluntary act; for a bolt of lightning to descend to earth is 'natural violence.' That the stroller should happen to be at the point struck by the flash is 'fortune.' Such fortune can be good or evil, according as it benefits or harms a man." See Green, II, 287-88.

47. Charles Trinkaus, "Humanism, Religion, Society: Concepts and Motivations of Some Recent Studies," *Renaissance Quarterly,* 29 (1976), 692.

48. Joseph Harris, " 'Maiden in the Mor Lay' and the Medieval Magdalene Tradition," *Journal of Medieval and Renaissance Studies,* 1 (1971), 70.

49. *Ibid.,* p. 74.

50. Cf. Cervantes's tale *La Gitanilla* (The Little Gypsy Girl), in which the author breaks in upon his narrative to warn his protagonist: "Mind what you've said, Preciosa, and what you are going to say.... Do you want visible proof, girls? Well, look there and you'll see that he's fainted in his chair.... Go up to him straight away ... and bring him round again." Cited from the translation by C. A. Jones (Harmondsworth: Penguin, 1972), p. 48.

51. Cited by Neal Wood, "Some Common Aspects of the Thought of Seneca and Machiavelli," *Renaissance Quarterly,* 21 (1968), 16-17. This concept is repeated throughout Seneca's writings. See my *The Valencian Dramatists* ...., pp. 119-24.

52. Wood, p. 15.

53. See Aristotle, *Poetics,* 24:1: "Furthermore, epic poetry must divide into the same types as tragedy, that is, the simple, the complex, that which turns on character, and that which turns on suffering."

54. With particular reference to the Spanish *comedia* and the relationship of the Valencians (including Virués) to the so-called creator Lope, see the previously cited work by Froldi and my own cited *The Valencian Dramatists....* Of interest are reviews of these two volumes by the same scholar, J. G. Fucilla who, in *Hispania,* 47 (1964), 867, wrote of Froldi's book, "Has Mr. Froldi through the presentation of historical evidence succeeded in vanquishing the myths that have prevailed about Lope and the creation of the *comedia?* His arguments are very convincing." In the intervening years, Fucilla appears to have been convinced, for there is no interrogative in his review of my book, in *Hispania,* 60 (1977), 391: "The youthful Lope, who lived in Valencia in 1589-90, could hardly have escaped being influenced by this trend [of the honor code] as well as in matters of the style and structure of his *comedias.*" The relevance to the matter at hand in our present text is not the question of who originated which genre but that of the cultural ambience in which any art is produced.

55. Cf. the review of Carroll B. Johnson's *Matías de los Reyes and the*

Craft of Fiction, by F. P. Casa in *Hispanic Review,* 44 (1976), 87: "The works of minor writers have always held a particular attraction for the scholar. They offer an opportunity ... to provide a meaningful contrast to the production of major figures. There is the hope that if we deal with works that are not infused with the greatness of genius, the mysterious process of the literary creation will be revealed to us."

Chapter Three

1. *A Definition of Tragedy,* pp. 103-104. For a useful description of how we can become trapped by preconceived notions of the definition of tragedy, see A. A. Parker, *"El médico de su honra* as Tragedy," *Hispanófila,* special issue, no. 2 (1975), pp. 3-5.
2. *Lope de Vega y la formación de la comedia,* p. 113.
3. All references to the five dramas by Virués are taken from vol. I of the previously cited edition by Eduardo Juliá Martínez.
4. That the denouement is not a given moment but a process of some duration is emphasized in my previously cited book, *Hacia la Comedia.*
5. Sargent, pp. 116-17.
6. *Ibid.,* p. 55.
7. Compare: "I am the Duchess of Malfi still" (Webster, *The Duchess of Malfi*); "I am Antony yet" (Shakespeare, *Antony and Cleopatra*).
8. *La tragedia en el renacimiento español,* p. 483.
9. *Ibid.*
10. *Ibid.*
11. *Spanish Drama Before Lope de Vega,* p. 183. It needs to be pointed out, given the many other deaths in Virués's dramas and the importance of this detail in assessing Virués's conception of theatrical decorum, that Crawford errs in believing Dido's suicide to take place "in the presence of her suitor." She is already dead when the doors are opened in Iarbas's presence (p. 175). Crawford's misreading may be the result of having mistaken Dido's last words (a recitation of some six dozen hendecasyllabic lines) to have been spoken by her, when in fact they are in the form of a letter which is read aloud by one of Dido's advisers.
12. *Woman and Society in the Spanish Drama . . . ,* p. 65.
13. *Ibid.,* p. 64. Cf. Sargent, p. 99, who speaks of "the other Virués superwomen: Dido, Semiramis, Casandra, even Felina...."
14. On the implications for the drama of the characters' virility, see my *The Valencian Dramatists . . . ,* pp. 118-32. See also the McKendrick book cited above, as well as my review of it in *Bulletin of the Comediantes,* 27 (1975), 141-46.
15. This paragraph of the present book draws freely on observations made in my *The Valencian Dramatists . . . ,* pp. 34-35.
16. She maintains that "the matter must depend on free will" (p. 147), a clear indication that Iarbas's demand for marriage requires a response

on a level in addition to that of the vow of chastity.

17. Virués himself tells us so, as we pointed out in chapter 1.

18. In addition to being included in the editions of Virués's works (Madrid, 1609 and Madrid, 1929), *La gran Semíramis* was published separately (London-Edinburgh-Leipzig, 1858), included in an anthology, *Selección de comedias del Siglo de Oro español,* ed. A. V. Ebersole (Madrid: Castalia, 1973), and most recently included (in a very abridged version of act III) in another collection, *Antología de la literatura española,* ed. J. M. Diez Borque (Madrid: Biblioteca Universitaria Guadiana, 1975).

19. *Woman and Society in the Spanish Drama...,* p. 64.

20. Of the several comments which reveal that the attempted deification of Semíramis is not successful, the clearest is that spoken by the servant Diarco: "Can there be anything to equal this! Don't you notice the lie / with which he orders his mother's death?" (p. 56).

21. Terms like "necessary" and "inescapable" are used here not for their pejorative connotations but because, as was pointed out in the preface, it is not my purpose in this volume to deal in depth with the one aspect of Virués's works that has been treated at length by all those who have written of him, namely tragedy. It will become increasingly obvious to the reader of the present book that I find the insistence upon seeing these dramas as tragedies not a fruitful path to follow. This posture should not be confused with a refutation of such analyses; most certainly the detailed study by Hermenegildo is not only valuable as a critical evaluation of Virués's works but illuminating with respect to Virués's place in the general attempt to develop tragedy in sixteenth-century Spain. What I do wish to stress here, as suggested in the preface, is that a more rewarding path to follow is to relegate to the background the unilateral analysis as tragedy, so that we may see something else emerging. By "something else" I mean neither tragedy, nontragedy, nor pseudotragedy but, in accord with my stated purpose, a transitional, pivotal artistic activity, the details of which do indeed form the substance of this book.

Although he makes reference to what he calls "the Valencian tragedians," I am in agreement with C. A. Jones in his previously cited "Tragedy in the Spanish Golden Age," when he suggests that "the concern to trace signs of classical tragedy, or indeed of tragedy at all, may lead us to lose sight of what seem to me the much broader concerns of the Spanish dramatists of the Golden Age...." (p. 102).

22. Cited from the translation by Gerald F. Else, *op. cit.,* p. 18.

23. Bernard Weinberg, "Robortello on the *Poetics,*" in *Critics and Criticism,* ed. R. S. Crane (Chicago: Univ. of Chicago Press, 1975), p. 331.

24. *Ibid.,* Cf. Lope de Vega's paraphrase of the same passage (admittedly via Robortello): "...comedy being different from tragedy in that it treats of lowly and plebeian actions, and tragedy of royal and great ones."

(Brewster translation cited in note 46 to our chapter 1.)

25. A. A. Parker, "Towards a Definition of Calderonian Tragedy," *Bulletin of Hispanic Studies*, 39 (1962), 222-37.

26. *Woman and Society in the Spanish Drama...*, p. 68.

27. Sargent, p. 133. The "obvious intentions" of Virués are adduced by Sargent from the prologues and epilogues, a subject to which we shall return in chapter 5. For the matter at hand, cf. Leicester Bradner, "From Petrarch to Shakespeare," in *The Renaissance* (New York: Harper & Row, 1962), p. 113: "If a tragedy is to achieve high rank it must convince us that the character whose fall is depicted had elements of greatness in him."

28. *Ibid.*, p. 129.

29. McKendrick, p. 68. It is difficult to understand why Semíramis's promiscuity is described as latent. In addition to the matters alluded to in our summary of this play, Semíramis herself tells us that she is determined to seduce Zopiro, considering such sexual activity her recreation (p. 38). Later, wearing her son's clothing, she says that her identity will be known only by "the one who undresses me, and that will be Zopiro" (p. 45). We subsequently learn that she had killed "more than a thousand young men with whom she satisfied her blind appetite, seducing each one in a single night or a single day in her lascivious bed" (p. 53).

30. Most scholars are in agreement with respect to the dominant themes: ambition and courtly intrigue. Hermenegildo has carried this one step further by perceiving a parallel between such situations and the assassination of Juan de Escobedo, secretary to Don Juan of Austria, allegedly at the instigation of the princess of Eboli and by the hand of Antonio Pérez. In his review of Hermenegildo's *La tragedia en el renacimiento español* (in *Bulletin of the Comediantes*, 27 [1975], 130-36), R. R. MacCurdy discusses what he calls Hermenegildo's "intriguing" and "appealing, though unprovable, thesis." MacCurdy succinctly summarizes how "in *La gran Semíramis* [Hermenegildo] detects allusions to the conspiracy of Antonio Pérez and the Princes[s] of Eboli against Philip's throne, because Semíramis like the Princess, captures the will of the king (Nino = Philip II) before setting off on her own destructive path" (p. 133). My purpose in citing MacCurdy is to underscore that Hermenegildo's interpretation, as well as MacCurdy's evaluation, necessarily share an assumption which is fundamental to my own point of departure. if Semíramis, *like the princess of Eboli*, "captures the will of the king," we can scarcely take seriously any interpretation which requires "fate" to place her in such a position. Clearly her own machinations have brought her to this point, as our text elaborates.

31. We have here another example of manner in contrast to outcome. The Semíramis legend is hardly original with Virués (a full treatment of the sources is found in Sargent, pp. 68-75), and the poet could assume sufficient knowledge on the part of the audience to anticipate base qualities in the protagonist. If he did doubt it, he left room for little else when in

his brief prologue he informed the audience that they were about to see a work about "the life and death of great Semíramis, / tyrannical queen of great Assyria" (p. 25). For a thorough study of the sources not only prior to and including the Virués play, but through Calderón's *La hija del aire,* see Gwynne Edwards, "Calderón's *La hija del aire* in the Light of His Sources," *Bulletin of Hispanic Studies,* 43 (1966), 177-96, as well as Edwards's introduction to his edition of the Calderón play (London: Tamesis, 1970). See also Angel Valbuena Briones, *Perspectiva crítica de los dramas de Calderón* (Madrid: Rialp, 1965), pp. 230-38.

32. In *The Valencian Dramatists...*, p. 129, I suggested that "of the virtues, fortitude, not justice, had primacy in the Valencian *comedias* and this explains why so very frequently it is the *struggle,* the need to exhibit *strength,* that forms the central point of the *comedias.*" I had in mind, of course, these virtues in their dramatic function as *motifs* of the plays (rather than as any reflection of the ultimate primacy in a social scale of values, in which case the exercise of fortitude was naturally viewed with an eye toward preserving or restoring justice). It should come as no surprise to those familiar with the Spanish *comedia* generally, that one could make a similar case for prudence, provided we have in mind what Maritain so aptly defined: "Thus prudence, the moral virtue par excellence (I mean old *prudentia* in its genuine sense, practical wisdom at the highest degree of practicality, the virtue through which the Bold make an infallible decision, not our bourgeois and timorous prudence) — prudence is the straight intellectual determination of actions to be done." (*Creative Intuition in Art and Poetry* [New York: Pantheon, 1953], p. 48.) The passage in *Great Semíramis* to which this note refers confirms this meaning of "prudence" not only because it is linked with "fortitude" but because of the context in which both words are found, i.e., amid battlefield conditions and following upon a military siege.

33. Cf. Mérimée, *L'Art dramatique à Valencia,* p. 344. who points out that Semíramis barely objects to her abduction, accompanying her "ravisher" after a timid protest of three words.

34. "Willful spirit" is my rendition of the Spanish *ánimo.*

35. Hermenegildo, p. 227, observes: "The one and the other are, in reality, but the scenic reduplication of one single personage."

36. *Ibid.,* p. 230.

37. The critics vary with respect to the intensity of religious feeling in the dramas as compared to the epic poem. Sargent (pp. 44-45) avers: "For the fundamental quality in Virués is religious sentiment. He is not deeply spiritual; there is little of the mystic about him. But the quality that colors his whole life is nevertheless religious enthusiasm; it determined his career as a soldier; it breathes through all his work as a poet. The *Monserrate* is rooted in piety.... Even in the plays where the pagan subject-matter precludes direct expression of Christian sentiments, we find constant appeal to a righteous Providence...." Hermenegildo warns us to "understand

Notes and References

well that what [Virués] preaches is purely a natural morality. If the Christian religiosity of the Valencian captain was patent in his poem *Monserrate*, in the tragedies, and in this one [*Cassandra*] particularly, such a religious sentiment was totally forgotten" (*La tragedia en el renacimiento español,* pp. 243-44).

38. The point requires emphasis because it is easy to confuse ethical and dramatic purposes. In an otherwise favorable review of my *The Valencian Dramatists...,* J. G. Fucilla (*Hispania*, 60 [1977], 392) suggests a contradiction on my part "by conceding that the 'second life,' the life of fame, dominates the [honor] concept as compared with the 'third life,' eternal life, which hardly makes an appearance in the *comedias*...." This is in fact precisely the point being made in that volume, namely that although hierarchically speaking, the "interjection of a *second life*..., [is] of intermediate length and value between the mortal and immortal varieties of life" (p. 121), as a source of dramatic conflict, this so-called second life, or concern for worldly fame, was of greater importance. Similarly, in the passages we are analyzing in the present volume, moral and ethical considerations insist upon virtue and a concern for eternal verities as matters of ultimate consequence (the "moral" or "point" of the play which the author leaves with us as we leave the theater), but our interest in the intrigue, in the conflict, in the challenges which the play's characters must confront — in a word, in the *drama* — is kindled and sustained by temporal concerns. Rather than a contradiction, this phenomenon reveals a paradox which not infrequently lies at the heart of much post-medieval art. The lines about to be quoted in the main body of our text reflect what we have just said: the words very clearly stress the supremacy of the eternal life (symbolized by a "good" death) whereas the dramatic interest finds its importance in the temporal confrontations with the "rapid wheel" of fortune.

39. *L'Art dramatique à Valencia,* p. 346.

40. Sargent, p. 85.

41. *La tragedia en el renacimiento* español, pp. 233-34. Cf. Sargent, p. 86: "The play is the most complicated of the collection."

42. *The Valencian Dramatists...,* p. 44. The Atkinson quotation is from his cited "Séneca, Virués, Lope de Vega," p. 126.

43. Sargent, p. 86.

44. Consider an analogous approach in the field of music. A collection of overtures to Verdi's operas would include excerpts from relatively obscure works (although the overtures themselves may be familiar ones). A recent television program concentrated on familiar and successful songs from Broadway musicals that had failed. We may learn about the art of the opera or the musical comedy from an examination of what the composer was attempting to create even in the face of the ultimate artistic failure of the work as a whole. A beautiful song in an opera that is a flop remains just that: a beautiful song, fit for a recital where it may be appre-

ciated in a way related to yet different from its original purpose. In a parallel manner, an examination of the things Virués wished to say in *Cassandra* will not make a success of the play but may reveal the direction he was intending to pursue, which in turn may aid us in the comprehension of his works as a whole.

45. Sargent, p. 85. It is interesting to note that although it is agreed that *Cassandra* is not a great work of art, much of its failure is attributable to experimentation in what would later be better presented in abler hands, namely the blending of serious and comic elements, the multiple plot, the absence of the "disinterested spectator," the subordination of plot and character development to theme and exemplarity, etc.

46. *La tragedia en el renacimiento español,* p. 239.

47. *Ibid.,* p. 235.

48. Robert Brustein, dean of the Yale School of Drama, recently observed that the postmodernist movement of European drama questions that "cause A precedes consequence B, which in turn is responsible for catastrophe C." According to Brustein, these dramatists ask whether it is not possible that "events are so multiple and complicated that the human intelligence may never comprehend the full set of causes preceding any situation, consequence or feeling? The post-modernists, in short, have been attempting to repeal the fundamental law of cause-and-effect which had been an unquestioned statute at least since the Enlightenment — the law that rules the linear, logical, rationalistic world of literature and, in particular, the Western literature of guilt." This should not mean, of course, that all of us should rush to our bookshelves and trot out the most incomprehensible plays and "explain" them in this light. Nonetheless, a play as complex and apparently as indecipherable as *Cassandra* may be more easily apprehended if we bear in mind the following observation: "The drama of the Greeks and Elizabethans ... is rarely causal in our modern sense: Human motives are sometimes so numerous that latter-day commentators find it hard to give the characters credibility. Clytemnestra offers not one but five or six reasons for killing Agamemnon; Iago mentions so many motives for hating Othello that Coleridge was led to speak of a 'motiveless malignity'; and T. S. Eliot criticized Shakespeare for failing to give Hamlet an 'objective correlative,' meaning simply that he found Hamlet's feelings to be in excess of his situation." See Robert Brustein, "Drama in the Age of Einstein," *The New York Times,* 7 August 1977, sect. 2, p. 1.

49. Sargent, p. 85.

50. McKendrick, p. 63.

51. *Ibid.,* p. 64.

52. Crawford, p. 185. Cf. Hermenegildo, *La tragedia en el renacimiento español,* p. 237: "...another woman [who is] an authentic artist of crime."

53. The implication is that the ascending motion of the wheel of fortune

has carried her plans so high as to be approaching the moon's halo of brightness. Virués employs the same image once more in *Unhappy Marcela* (see our chapter 4, section V). Cf. the 1726 *Diccionario de autoridades,* which quotes a quatrain from the *Rimas* of a younger contemporary of Virués, the prince of Esquilache, Francisco de Borja (1581-1658), to illustrate this meaning. An English rendition would be:

> May I be lifted by the wheel of fortune
> without halts or beats to the high summit;
> may it forget a while its normal habit,
> until it's raised me to the halo of the moon.

54. Sargent, p. 87.
55. Sargent, pp. 89-97, provides an exhaustive treatment of sources and influences upon the Virués play.
56. That the destructive power of erotic love as one of the principal causes of human miseries is a fundamental and pervasive theme in Virués's works has been shown by Sargent throughout her book. We should recall its role in the *Monserrate* as well.
57. *La tragedia en el renacimiento español,* p. 258.
58. C. S. Lewis, *The Discarded Image,* p. 140.
59. "From Petrarch to Shakespeare," pp. 114-15.

Chapter Four

1. See note 62 to our chapter 1. We should also recall that Lope's reference to Virués's plays as *tragedias* has itself been used as an authoritative basis for distinguishing them from *comedias*. See note 61 to our chapter 1.
2. See *History of Spanish Literature,* II, 77. Note once more how readily the word "absurd" is used to describe Virués's plays. For yet another example, see George T. Northup, *An Introduction to Spanish Literature,* revised by Nicholson B. Adams (Chicago: Univ. of Chicago Press, 1960), p. 242: "Cristóbal de Virués outdid Cueva in sensationalism, carrying this tendency to the point of absurdity."
3. Ticknor, II, 77-78.
4. Frederick Bouterwek, *History of Spanish Literature* (London, 1847), p. 313. Cited by Sargent, p. 143 n. Elsewhere (p. 153 n), Sargent cites Bouterwek's opinion that Virués was "born for tragic art."
5. Sargent, pp. 153-54
6. *Ibid.*, p. 154, Cf. Gwynne Edwards, "Calderón's *La hija del aire* in the Light of His Sources," p. 184, who observes that Virués "remains in accord with the conventions of the *comedia* in his concern with moral issues and their illustration through specific themes.... In relation to the source material, Virués' significant contribution, therefore, was one of

organizing and reshaping something loose and episodic in order to develop certain themes. In this respect he is a clear forerunner of the great Golden Age dramatists...." The substance of this observation is accurate, but we note another curious ambivalence: if Virués is "a clear forerunner" for reasons of chronology, how can he be described as *remaining* "in accord with the conventions of the *comedia*" when these conventions presumably had yet to be firmly established?

7. *Historia del teatro español,* I, 116.
8. *La tragedia en el renacimiento español,* p. 263.
9. *Lope de Vega y la formación de la comedia,* pp. 113-14.
10. *Spanish Drama Before Lope de Vega,* p. 185.
11. Alan S. Trueblood, *Experience and Artistic Expression in Lope de Vega: The Making of "La Dorotea"* (Cambridge, Mass.: Harvard Univ. Press, 1974), p. 347. On Bermúdez's chronology, see M. D. Triwedi, "Notas para una biografía de Jerónimo Bermúdez," *Hispanófila,* 29 (1967), 1-9.
12. *Historia de la literatura española,* II, 783.
13. *El teatro español en su Siglo de Oro,* p. 75. The comment on shutting up precepts under lock and key is a reference to Lope's statement in the *New Art* that he had shut up the precepts with six keys. Not unlike Valbuena's judgment is Hermenegildo's reference to the function of liaison, of bridge, of advancement toward Lope, which the Virués theatre has (*La tragedia en el renacimiento español,* p. 215), although he insists (accurately, we may add) that Virués was unable to come up with the definitive formula. By this he means what has come to be known as the Lopean formula for the Spanish *comedia,* but it is well to remember that in the late sixteenth century Lope himself had yet to hit upon "his" formula, a point emphasized by Frida Weber de Kurlat in a paper (delivered at the sixth congress of the Asociación Internacional de Hispanistas in Toronto, August 1977) titled "Lope-Lope y Lope-pre-Lope...," by which is meant the distinction between the Lope de Vega who was master of the formula dominated by his approach and the earlier experimental Lope who was still toying with a variety of approaches.
14. Although Virués is generally considered to have been fond of deaths in his dramas, Tersilo's death is neither presented nor explicitly related. Aside from the general interpretation we should make of this, namely, that the poet's penchant for deaths is not an invariable characteristic of his art, the particular death of Tersilo has importance for our understanding of the honor concept as Virués conceived it. See my *The Valencian Dramatists...,* pp. 45-46. As for the question of whether Tersilo did in fact die, Sargent and Hermenegildo both refer to his being taken to Santiago to be cared for, Sargent subsequently referring to "the unexplained dropping out of the action of Tersilo" (*op. cit.,* p. 107). I agree with Mérimée (*op. cit.,* p. 348) that Tersilo did die, as is shown in my analysis of the honor problem in the work cited above.

15. Sargent (p. 101) calls Felina the wife of Formio. There is nothing to confirm the formality of the relationship. Mérimée (p. 349) calls her simply "a woman of his band," and Hermenegildo, in his 1961 volume (p. 595) as well as in his 1973 work (p. 591), describes her as Formio's lover, and occasionally as the prostitute who accompanies the bandits. For a discussion of Formio's and Felina's social class, see my article, "Nobility in the Theater of Virués," *Romance Notes,* 7 (1966), 180–82.

16. *El teatro español en su Siglo de Oro,* p. 76.

17. First noted as such by S. G. Morley, "Strophes in the Spanish Drama Before Lope de Vega," in *Homenaje ofrecido a Menéndez Pidal* (Madrid, 1925), I, 523. Of the many others who have mentioned the priority, only Porrata qualifies the observation by suggesting that Virués was only "one of the first to use *romance* strophe in a theatrical work." See Francisco Porrata, *Incorporación del romancero a la temática de la comedia española* (Madrid: Plaza Mayor, 1972).

18. William E. Wilson, *Guillén de Castro* (New York: Twayne, 1973), p. 37.

19. Atkinson, p. 127.

20. *La tragedia en el renacimiento español,* p. 591. The *quintilla* is a strophe of five octosyllabic lines with a variety of rhyme schemes. Contrary to Hermenegildo's comment about *Marcela,* there are no *quintillas* in this work; however, they are found in *Semíramis* and *Atila.* See Mérimée's "Tableau des mètres employés par Virués" (*L'Art dramatique à Valencia,* pp. 360–61).

21. *La tragedia en el renacimiento español,* p. 260.

22. *Ibid.,* p. 266.

23. *Ibid.,* p. 262. (The statement is also found in *Los trágicos españoles del siglo XVI,* pp. 261–62.)

24. *La tragedia en el renacimiento español,* p. 262. Cf. *ibid.,* p. 261: "This work is the author's last degree of evolution toward the modern theater."

25. Virués's contemporary and fellow Valencian, Andrés Rey de Artieda, is only one of several who sought inspiration in the Italian authors. His one extant play, *Los amantes,* not only combines a Spanish legend with Classical motifs, but relies on Boccaccio and, as Fucilla has recently suggested, on Petrarch as well. Moreover, he praised Ariosto as the "divine."

26. Othón Arróniz, *La influencia italiana en el nacimiento de la comedia española* (Madrid: Gredos, 1969), pp. 70–71.

27. Sargent herself writes in the very next sentence: "To lend the tragic touch to such portions of the *Orlando Furioso* as he had selected for his play, Virués had to invent new parts."

28. *Los trágicos españoles del siglo XVI,* p. 262; *La tragedia en el renacimiento español,* p. 263.

29. See note 15 above.

30. *La tragedia en el renacimiento español,* p. 264.
31. *Ibid.*
32. *Ibid.,* p. 265.
33. *Woman and Society in the Spanish Drama...,* pp. 62-63.
34. Even here, Dido's position as monarch is the result of her brother's having murdered her husband Siqueo. Though it would be stretching a point to insist on this detail as being in accord with what we shall observe in the other four dramas, particularly since Virués was drawing upon well known sources, the fact remains that he did not need to — it is revealed in narratives and not as an essential part of the action of the play — and so Virués *chose* to remind us that it was murder which removed the king from the throne and placed a strong-willed person (albeit legitimately) on the throne as protagonist of our play.
35. Northrop Frye, *Anatomy of Criticism* (Princeton: Princeton Univ. Press, 1971), p. 187.
36. Arnold Hauser, *The Social History of Art* (New York: Random House, 1951), II, 99-100.
37. *Ibid.,* p. 103.
38. See our chapter 3, note 53.
39. Arnold G. Reichenberger, "Thoughts About Tragedy in the Spanish Theater of the Golden Age," *Hispanófila,* special issue, no. 1 (1974), p. 42. The translated lines of Lope's play are taken from the edition of W. F. King (Lincoln, Neb.: Univ. of Nebraska Press, 1972).
40. *La tragedia en el renacimiento español,* p. 263.
41. *Woman and Society in the Spanish Drama...,* p. 70.
42. On fortitude and prudence, see note 32 to our chapter 3.
43. See *Don Quixote,* I, 12-14.
44. See my *The Valencian Dramatists...,* pp. 119-24.
45. On Rojas, see especially R. R. MacCurdy, *Francisco de Rojas Zorrilla and the Tragedy* (Albuquerque: Univ. of New Mexico Press, 1958) and, among others, MacCurdy's introduction to the Clásicos Castellanos edition of two of Rojas's plays.

Chapter Five

1. Barbara Herrnstein Smith, *Poetic Closure* (Chicago: Univ. of Chicago Press, 1968), p. 152. For an intriguing explanation of why we are interested in endings generally (as they relate to our human concern with our own end), see Frank Kermode, *The Sense of an Ending* (London: Oxford Univ. Press, 1966).
2. Alberto Porqueras Mayo, *El prólogo como género literario* (Madrid: C.S.I.C., 1957), p. 72.
3. *Ibid.,* p. 54.
4. I am translating the "entirety" of the prologue as it appears on p. 503 of the edition used throughout my chapter 2. This edition does not in-

clude the final lines, which constitute an explanation of Virués's orthography. Given the purpose of the present book, a discussion of Virués's spelling of Spanish seems irrelevant. The curious reader may consult a copy of the early editions as described in our bibliography, or the appendix of Sargent's book which reproduces this portion of the prologue and adds some clarifying commentary.

5. *La tragedia en el renacimiento español,* p. 210. See also John G. Weiger, "A Humanist Echo in Virués's *Monserrate,*" *Romance Notes,* forthcoming.

6. Américo Castro's work, *De la edad conflictiva,* bears a title difficult to translate, particularly inasmuch as the word *conflictiva,* despite its evident English cognate, is not registered by the dictionary of the Royal Spanish Academy. That this has been readily accepted is more than a tribute to Castro's authority: it as well testifies to the appropriateness of a word which suggests more than conflict; hence my rendition in the text.

7. Albareda, *op. cit.*

8. The matter is most often discussed in relation to *Don Quixote.* See, for instance, Bruce W. Wardropper, "*Don Quijote:* Story or History?" *Modern Philology,* 43 (1965), 1-11.

9. *Don Quixote,* I, 1.

10. *The Discarded Image,* pp. 208-209.

11. *Ibid.,* p. 210. Cf. Lewis's earlier statement: "To the best of my knowledge no medieval author mentions either faculty [Phantasy or Imagination] as a characteristic of poets. If they had been given to talking about poets in any way at all — they usually talk only of their language or their learning — I think they would have used *invention* where we use *imagination*" (*ibid.,* pp. 162-63). See also Hauser, *op. cit.,* II, 69: "This idea [of genius] remained foreign to the Middle Ages, which recognized no independent value in intellectual originality and spontaneity, recommended the imitation of the masters, and considered plagiarism permissible...." For a less equivocal declaration by Virués concerning his originality in the epic, see his verses cited in note 49 to our chapter 1.

12. Ernst Robert Curtius, *European Literature and the Latin Middle Ages,* trans. W. R. Trask (Princeton: Princeton Univ. Press, 1973), pp. 85-89.

13. *El prólogo como género literario,* p. 141.

14. Curtius, p. 86.

15. I have modernized the spelling of Virués's given name. The original spelling may be found in the Bibliography. Virués's title page also reflects the primary importance accorded to the dramatic works, since it refers the reader to the list of titles to be found on the following page: *Tabla de las Tragedias que en este libro se contienen.*

16. See Milton's *Paradise Lost,* 3:412-14.

17. *The Valencian Dramatists...,* pp. 32, 38, 39.

18. My observation must be qualified as a generalization, but it is based

on such well-known declarations as Cervantes's assertion that "blood is inherited but virtue is acquired, and virtue by itself alone has a worth that blood does not have" (*Don Quixote,* II, 43), which must be contrasted with Lope's contention that "no man is honored by himself, for honor is received by one man from another.... For a man to be virtuous and meritorious is not to be *honrado*.... From which it is clear that honor is in another and not in himself" (*Los comendadores de Córdoba*).

19. Hermenegildo, *La tragedia en el renacimiento español,* pp. 259-60, sees in this prologue evidence of Virués's progress toward seventeenth-century sensibilities, particularly in the representation of Cupid devoid of the poetic and idealistic halo of the Renaissance.

20. In a private conversation after the session, Professor Parker agreed that the Virués prologue may indeed be the basis for this attribute of many *comedias.* Professor Valbuena added that such a structure is particularly characteristic of the plays known as *comedias de santos.*

21. *La tragedia en el renacimiento español,* p. 261.

Selected Bibliography

PRIMARY SOURCES

1. The *Monserrate*

El Monserrate de Cristóval de Virués. Madrid: Querino Gerardo, 1587. The *editio princeps,* printing of which continued into 1588, accounting for the discrepancy in various bibliographies. Copies exist in the Biblioteca Nacional de Madrid, the British Museum, and the Hispanic Society of America.

El Monserrate segundo. Milan: Gratiadio Ferioli, 1602. A revised edition of the poem, some strophes having been changed and many new ones added. The inaccessibility is dramatized by Rosell's spelling of the Italian publisher as "Ferrioll," and by Martí Grajales's version of "Frioli." The copy in the library of the monastery of Montserrat spells it as given here.

El Monserrate, tercera impressión añadida y notablemente mejorada. Madrid: Alonso Martín, 1609.

El Monserrate. Ed. Agustín Bonacasa y Castro. Madrid: Sancha, 1805.

El Monserrate. Ed. Cayetano Rosell. In *Poemas épicos,* I (Biblioteca de Autores Españoles, 17). 1849. Reprint. Madrid: Ediciones Atlas, 1945. This is the text utilized for the excerpts quoted in the present volume.

2. Plays

Obras trágicas y líricas del Capitán Cristóval de Virués. Madrid: Alonso Martín, 1609. Although speculation exists concerning an earlier edition, this remains generally acknowledged to be the *editio princeps.* The edition contains the five dramas of Virués in the following order: *La gran Semíramis, La cruel Casandra, Atila furioso, La infelice Marcela, Elisa Dido,* followed in turn by Virués's lyric poetry. Copies exist in the Biblioteca Nacional de Madrid, the Rennert Collection of the University of Pennsylvania Library, the Ticknor Collection of the Boston Public Library, and the Hispanic Society of America.

La gran Semíramis. London, Edinburgh, and Leipzig: Williams and Norgate, 1858. Münch describes this book as having been published only in London and Edinburgh, somewhat curious since he himself was

German and published his study only two years later in Berlin. Mérimée describes this edition as having been published only in Leipzig but with a preface in English. The edition was printed in Leipzig but published in Britain.

Poetas dramáticos valencianos. Edited by Eduardo Juliá Martínez. 2 vols. Madrid: Real Academia Española, 1929. Vol. I contains the five Virués plays, as well as an important introduction of 135 pages concerning the Valencian dramatists, the section devoted to Virués comprising twelve of them.

La gran Semíramis. In *Selección de comedias del Siglo de Oro español.* Edited with an introduction by Alva V. Ebersole. Madrid: Editorial Castalia, 1973. (Estudios de Hispanófila, 24.)

La gran Semíramis. In *Antología de la literatura española: Teatro de los siglos XVI y XVII.* Edited by José María Diez Borque. Madrid: Biblioteca Universitaria Guadiana, 1975. Pp. 185-88 contain vv. 741-868 of the third act of *La gran Semíramis,* the acknowledged source being the Ebersole anthology.

SECONDARY SOURCES

ALBAREDA, ANSELM M. *Historia de Montserrat.* Revised and enlarged by Josep Massot i Muntaner. Barcelona: Publicacions de l'Abadia de Montserrat, 1974. The most complete account of Montserrat and its monastery, this carefully documented work prides itself on its factual accuracy, specifically devoid of the Garín legend.

ARISTOTLE. *Poetics.* Translated by Gerald F. Else. Ann Arbor: Univ. of Michigan Press, 1970. (Ann Arbor Paperbacks.)

ATKINSON, WILLIAM C. Séeneca, Virués, Lope de Vega." In *Homenatge a Antoni Rubió i Lluch.* Barcelona: Estudis Universitaris Catalans, 1936, I, 111-31. Represents Virués as the link between Seneca and Lope in the development of the Spanish drama.

AUERBACH, ERICH. *Mimesis: The Representation of Reality in Western Literature.* Translated by W. R. Trask. Princeton: Princeton Univ. Press, 1968.

BRADNER, LEICESTER. "From Petrarch to Shakespeare." In *The Renaissance,* pp. 97-119. New York: Harper & Row, 1962.

BRAUDEL, FERNAND. *The Mediterranean and the Mediterranean World in the Age of Philip II.* Translated by Siân Reynolds. 2 vols. New York: Harper & Row, 1973. A thought-provoking reevaluation of the historical background of the age in which Virués lived, fought, and wrote.

BRUSTEIN, ROBERT. "Drama in the Age of Einstein." *The New York Times,* 7 August 1977, sect. 2, p. 1.

BULFINCH, THOMAS. *The Age of Fable or Beauties of Mythology.* Edited by E. E. Hale. Boston: S. W. Tilton, 1881. A standard work.

Selected Bibliography

CAMPBELL, JOSEPH. *The Hero with a Thousand Faces.* 2nd edition. Princeton: Princeton Univ. Press, 1972. (Bollingen Series, XVII.)

CASA, FRANK P. Review of *Matías de los Reyes and the Craft of Fiction,* by Carroll B. Johnson. *Hispanic Review,* 44 (1976), 87–88.

CASTRO, AMERICO. *De la edad conflictiva: El drama do la honra en España y en su literatura.* Madrid: Taurus Ediciones, 1963.

CERVANTES SAAVEDRA, MIGUEL DE. *Don Quixote de la Mancha.* Translated by Samuel Putnam. 2 vols. New York: Viking Press, 1949. Also available in the Modern Library series published by Random House. One of the best renditions in English.

──────. *La Galatea.* Edited by Juan Bautista Avalle-Arce. 2 vols. Madrid: Espasa-Calpe, 1961. (Clásicos Castellanos, 154–55.)

──────. *Obras completas.* Edited by Angel Valbuena Prat. Madrid: Aguilar, 1965.

CIRLOT, J. E. *A Dictionary of Symbols.* Translated by Jack Sage from the Spanish *Diccionario de símbolos tradicionales.* New York: Philosophical Library, 1962.

CODINA Y FARRÉ, MIGUEL A. *Origen de la Virgen de Montserrat.* Barcelona: n.p., 1924.

CORNET Y MAS, CAYETANO. *Tres días en Montserrat: Guía histórico-descriptiva de todo cuanto contiene y encierra esta montaña.* Barcelona: Librería del Plus Ultra, 1858.

CRAWFORD, J. P. WICKERSHAM. *Spanish Drama Before Lope de Vega.* 2nd revised edition, 1937. Reprinted with corrections and bibliographical supplement by Warren T. McCready, Philadelphia: Univ. of Pennsylvania Press, 1967. A fundamental work for the study of the theater in Spain through the sixteenth century. Some five pages are devoted to Virués.

CURTIUS, ERNST ROBERT. *European Literature and the Latin Middle Ages.* Translated by Willard R. Trask. Bollingen Series, 36. Princeton: Princeton Univ. Press, 1973. A standard reference for scholars concerned with the development and coherence of the neo-Latin literatures. Especially useful for its discussion of *topoi.*

DEMETRIUS. *On Style.* Translated by W. Rhys Roberts, Cambridge: Harvard Univ. Press, 1932. (Loeb Classical Library, 199.)

Documents of the Christian Church. Selected and edited by Henry Bettenson. New York: Oxford Univ. Press, 1947.

DUNLAP, RHODES. "The Allegorical Interpretation of Renaissance Literature." *PMLA,* 82 (1967), 39–43.

ELLIOT, J. H. *Europe Divided: 1559–1598.* New York: Harper & Row, 1968.

──────. *Imperial Spain: 1469–1716.* New York: Mentor Books, 1966. A compendious and highly readable history of the period.

FERNÁNDEZ DE MORATÍN, LEANDRO. *Catálogo histórico y crítico de piezas dramáticas anteriores a Lope de Vega.* In *Obras de D. Nicolás y de D.*

Leandro Fernández de Moratín. Madrid: Atlas, 1944. (Biblioteca de Autores Españoles, 2). This volume includes the "Discurso histórico sobre los orígenes del teatro español."

FORCIONE, ALBAN K. *Cervantes, Aristotle, and the "Persiles."* Princeton: Princeton Univ. Press, 1970.

FROLDI, RINALDO. *Lope de Vega y la formación de la comedia.* Salamanca: Ediciones Anaya, 1968. Revised edition, translation by Franco Gabriel of the Italian *Il teatro valenzano e l'origine della commedia barocca* (Pisa: Editrice Tecnico-Scientifica, 1962). The seminal study with respect to the anticipatory role played by the Valencian dramatists in the evolution of the Spanish national drama. Emphasizes that the attribution of the genre exclusively to Lope de Vega is a Romantic myth.

FRYE, NORTHROP. *Anatomy of Criticism.* Princeton: Princeton Univ. Press, 1971.

FUCILLA, JOSEPH G. "Lope and Calderón's *La hija del aire*." *Bulletin of the Comediantes,* 27 (1975), 90–93. Discusses Lope's continuing attraction to the Semíramis legend, including a lost play by Lope and repeated references to Semíramis in nearly a dozen works of several genres by Lope.

———. Review of the original Italian edition of Froldi's work described above. *Hispania,* 47 (1964), 866–67.

———. Review of *The Valencian Dramatists of Spain's Golden Age,* by Weiger. *Hispania,* 60 (1977), 391-92.

GIRABAL, JOSÉ MARÍA. *Legends of Montserrat.* Translated by Joseph McKee. Barcelona: Editorial Balmes, 1974. Primarily intended for visitors to the monastery. Of an elementary and popular nature, this booklet is nonetheless a summary of many of the legends surrounding the mountain, including the Holy Grail and the Garín myth.

GREEN, OTIS H. "Sobre las dos Fortunas: De tejas arriba y de tejas abajo." In *Studia Philologica: Homenaje ofrecido a Dámaso Alonso por sus amigos y discípulos con ocasión de su 60.° aniversario.* Vol. II. Madrid: Gredos, 1961, pp. 143–54. Discusses the two kinds of fortune: worldly vicissitudes and divine providence.

———. *Spain and the Western Tradition: The Castilian Mind in Literature from "El Cid" to Calderón.* 4 vols. Madison: Univ. of Wisconsin Press, 1963-66.

HAMILTON, EDITH. *Mythology.* New York: New American Library, 1969. Less detailed than the Bulfinch work, a valuable and reliable compendium of mythological references.

HARRIS, JOSEPH. " 'Maiden in the Mor Lay' and the Medieval Magdalene Tradition." *Journal of Medieval and Renaissance Studies,* 1 (1971), 59–87.

HAUSER, ARNOLD. *The Social History of Art.* New York: Random House, 1951. 4 vols. (Vintage 114-17).

Selected Bibliography

HERMENEGILDO, ALFREDO. *La tragedia en el renacimiento español.* Barcelona: Planeta, 1973. Fundamentally and generally, these two works provide the same information. However, the 1973 volume is far better organized conceptually and although some entire sections are verbatim repetitions of the earlier work, the material on Virués has undergone a substantial and significant rethinking and consequent revision. Much previous scholarship, such as the English Crawford and Sargent contributions, is succinctly subsumed within this Spanish synthesis. An indispensable work for consultation on the tragic undercurrents of Spanish drama in the sixteenth century.

──────. *Los trágicos españoles del Siglo XVI.* Madrid: Fundación Universitaria Española, 1961.

HIGHET, GILBERT. *The Classical Tradition: Greek and Roman Influences on Western Literature.* London: Oxford Univ. Press, 1957.

JONES, C. A. "Tragedy in the Spanish Golden Age." In *The Drama of the Renaissance: Essays for Leicester Bradner.* Edited by Elmer M. Blistein. Providence: Brown Univ. Press, 1970, pp. 100-107. An insightful and concise evaluation of the concept as well as the label of tragedy as understood by Lope and Calderón. Many lengthier, more detailed (and better known) studies exist, but this compendious essay contains the essence of the problem and examines it lucidly.

LEWIS, C. S. *The Discarded Image: An Introduction to Medieval and Renaissance Literature.* London: Cambridge Univ. Press, 1967. Occasionally rhapsodic but highly readable excursion through the development of fundamental philosophical conceptions as expressed by writers before and through the period described in the title.

LONGINUS. *On the Sublime.* Translated by T. S. Dorsch. In *Classical Literary Criticism.* Harmondsworth: Penguin Books, 1965. Although the author's identity remains in doubt, the work contains a valuable exposition of rhetorical concepts.

LÓPEZ DE TORO, JOSÉ. *Los poetas de Lepanto.* Madrid: C.S.I.C., 1950.

LOVEJOY, ARTHUR O. *The Great Chain of Being: A Study of the History of an Idea.* Cambridge: Harvard Univ. Press, 1936.

MACCURDY, RAYMOND R. Review of *La tragedia en el renacimiento español,* by Hermenegildo. Not only a review of a work repeatedly cited in the present volume, but an essay in its own right which adds additional perspectives in a balanced and scholarly manner. *Bulletin of the Comediantes,* 27 (1975), 130-36.

MANDEL, OSCAR. *A Definition of Tragedy.* New York: New York University Press, 1961. (The Gotham Library.) A refreshing reexamination and reevaluation of a terminology and the concepts involved. The hero, free will, approaches to definitions and the distinction between tragic situations and tragic works in their totality are among the matters investigated.

MANRIQUE, JORGE. "Coplas por la muerte de su padre." In *Cancionero castellano del siglo XV.* Madrid: Bailly-Bailliere, 1915.

MARTÍ GRAJALES, FRANCISCO, ed. *Cancionero de la Academia de los Nocturnos de Valencia.* 4 vols. Valencia: Imprenta de Francisco Vives Mora, 1905-12. Modern edition with additions and notes of the 1869 edition compiled by Pedro Salvá. Includes poems by Jerónimo de Virués.

MARTÍ GRAJALES, FRANCISCO. *Ensayo de un diccionario biográfico y bibliográfico de los poetas que florecieron en el reino de Valencia hasta el año 1700.* Madrid: Revista de Archivos, Bibliotecas y Museos, 1927. A fundamental source of information on poets, major and minor, of Valencia through the seventeenth century. Biographies are given, precise bibliographical descriptions of editions are provided, and excerpts from relevant documents are included.

MCKENDRICK, MELVEENA. *Woman and Society in the Spanish Drama of the Golden Age: A Study of the "Mujer Varonil."* London: Cambridge Univ. Press, 1974. A highly perceptive study which provides much food for thought. The author's understanding of the role of the Valencian dramatists in the evolution of the national drama is out of date and the attempt to see feminist egalitarianism in every feminine character who displays characteristics conventionally associated with masculine personality traits is often forced.

MÉRIMÉE, HENRI. *L'Art dramatique à Valencia depuis les origines jusqu'au commencement du XVIIe siècle.* Toulouse: Imprimerie et Librairie Edouard Privat, 1913. The first work of any substance to deal with the drama in Valencia. A lengthy chapter deals with Virués and pp. 360-61 present a detailed analysis of the versification of each of the five dramas, act by act.

MORLEY, S. GRISWOLD, and COURTNEY BRUERTON. *Cronología de las comedias de Lope de Vega.* Madrid: Gredos, 1968. Translation, with revisions by Morley, of the original *The Chronology of Lope de Vega's Comedias* (New York: The Modern Language Association of America, 1940). A standard reference work.

MÜNCH-BELLINGHAUSEN, E. F. J. VON. "Virués Leben und Werke." In *Jahrbuch für romanische und englische Literatur,* II (1860), 139-63. A careful appraisal of Virués's works, including the lyric poems. Ticknor calls it a study "I should have been glad to have received earlier — before I had printed my account...."

PASTOR FUSTER, JUSTO. *Biblioteca valenciana de los escritores que florecieron hasta nuestros días.* Valencia: José Ximeno, 1827. Updates to the early nineteenth century the similar work by Vicente Ximeno.

PIERCE, FRANK. *The Heroic Poem of the Spanish Golden Age: Selections.* New York: Oxford Univ. Press, 1947. In addition to the four epic poems (abridged) that constitute the anthology, the concise introduction and the valuable notes to the selections are an aid for the reading of other Spanish epics of the Golden Age.

Selected Bibliography

———. *La poesía épica del Siglo de Oro.* Madrid: Gredos, 1968. A translation and expansion of Pierce's *Spanish Epic Poetry of the Golden Age.* Prepared with much care and based upon firm scholarship, an indispensable work. Contains a lengthy summary of previous scholarship on the Spanish epic of our period, a critical examination of the genre and most of its works (Virués is mentioned on some four dozen pages), and an extremely valuable and detailed set of appendices giving bibliographical descriptions.

PORQUERAS MAYO, ALBERTO. *El prólogo como género literario.* Madrid: C.S.I.C., 1957. An exhaustive study of the origin and development of the prologue from ancient times to the Spanish Golden Age. The author has also published anthologies of prologues, of which *El prólogo en el renacimiento español* (Madrid: C.S.I.C., 1965) is of particular relevance to our study.

REICHENBERGER, ARNOLD G. "Thoughts About Tragedy in the Spanish Theater of the Golden Age." *Hispanófila,* special issue, no. 1 (1974), 37–45.

RUIZ RAMÓN, FRANCISCO. *Historia del teatro español.* 2 vols. Madrid: Alianza Editorial, 1971.

SAMUELS, RICHARD S. "Benedetto Varchi, the *Accademia degli Infiammati,* and the Origins of the Italian Academic Movement." *Renaissance Quarterly,* 29 (1976), 599–633.

SÁNCHEZ, JOSÉ. *Academias literarias del Siglo de Oro español.* Madrid: Gredos, 1961.

SARGENT, CECILIA VENNARD. *The Dramatic Works of Cristóbal de Virués.* New York: Instituto de las Españas, 1930. Originally planned as a critical introduction to Virués's five plays, the appearance in 1929 of Juliá's *Poetas dramáticos valencianos* caused this work to appear as a monograph. The volume reflects much research, particularly with respect to sources for the plays, and is filled with insightful observations and intelligent interpretations. Indispensable for any study on Virués.

SINGLETON, CHARLES S., translator. *The Divine Comedy,* by Dante Alighieri. 3 vols., in two parts each. Princeton: Princeton Univ. Press, 1970–75.

SMITH, BARBARA HERNSTEIN. *Poetic Closure: A Study of How Poems End.* Chicago: Univ. of Chicago Press, 1968.

SPENCER, THEODORE. *Shakespeare and the Nature of Man.* New York: Macmillan, 1966.

TASSO, TORQUATO. *Jerusalem Delivered.* Translated [1600] by Edward Fairfax. New York: Capricorn Books, 1963.

TICKNOR, GEORGE. *History of Spanish Literature.* Sixth American edition, corrected and enlarged. 3 vols. New York: Gordian Press, 1965.

TILLYARD, E. M. W. *The Elizabethan World Picture.* New York: Random House Vintage Books, n.d. A concise study of the Renaissance views of the universe, particularly with regard to "the great chain of being."

TRINKAUS, CHARLES. "Humanism, Religion, Society: Concepts and Motivations of Some Recent Studies." *Renaissance Quarterly,* 29 (1976), 676–713.

VALBUENA BRIONES, ÁNGEL. *Perspectiva crítica de los dramas de Calderón.* Madrid: Ediciones Rialp, 1965.

VALBUENA PRAT, ÁNGEL. *Historia de la literatura española.* 3 vols. Barcelona: Editorial Gili, 1964.

―――. *El teatro español en su Siglo de Oro.* Barcelona: Planeta, 1969.

VALLVE, GRACIELA. "Drama of the Golden Age: The Tragedies of Cristóbal de Virués." Ph.D. dissertation in preparation, Emory University. Cited from Claude L. Hulet, "Dissertations in the Hispanic Languages and Literatures — 1974," *Hispania,* 58 (1975), 310–11.

VEGA, LOPE DE. *El arte nuevo de hacer comedias en este tiempo.* Edited with an introduction by Juana de José Prades. Madrid: C.S.I.C., 1971. Includes a reproduction of the Madrid 1613 edition and provides a line by line analysis and comparison with sources. A bibliography of works dealing with the poem is included, although some omissions inevitably occur, notably J. H. Parker's "Post-[Quadri]centennial Reflections," in *Hispanic Studies in Honor of N. B. Adams* (Chapel Hill: Univ. of North Carolina Press, 1966).

―――. *The New Art of Writing Plays.* Translation of the above by William T. Brewster, with an introduction by Brander Matthews. In *Papers on Playmaking.* New York: Hill and Wang, 1957, pp. 1–19.

WADE, GERALD E. Introduction to *El burlador de Sevilla y convidado de piedra,* by Tirso de Molina. New York: Charles Scribner's Sons, 1969, pp. 3–55. The introduction, as well as the notes, are more global in their applicability than most such items, and contribute to our linguistic and thematic understanding of the genre as well as the play of the edition.

WEIGER, JOHN G. *Hacia la Comedia: De los valencianos a Lope.* Madrid: Editorial Planeta, forthcoming. Virués is among those whose works are analyzed for their auditory qualities and for the relationship of the imagery employed to link opening and closing scenes.

―――. "A Humanist Echo in Virué's *Monserrate.*" *Romance Notes,* forthcoming. Attempts to place in a humanist context Virués's comparison of his monk's attitude to that of John Hus.

―――. "Lope's Role in the Lope de Vega Myth." *Hispania,* forthcoming. Suggests that Lope's references and reticences with respect to Virués can be related to the enhancement of Lope's legendary role as creator of the national *comedia.*

―――. "Nobility in the Theater of Virués." *Romance Notes,* 7 (1966), 180–82. Suggests that bandits in *La infelice Marcela* are of noble and possibly royal ancestry, thus explaining their language and behavior,

Selected Bibliography

both of which had seemed incongruous to some scholars.

———. Review of *Woman and Society in the Spanish Drama of the Golden Age: A Study of the "Mujer Varonil,"* by McKendrick. *Bulletin of the Comediantes,* 27 (1975), 141-46.

———. *The Valencian Dramatists of Spain's Golden Age.* Boston: Twayne, 1976. (Twayne's World Authors Series, 371) Chapter 3 is devoted to the dramas of Virués with particular emphasis on the honor theme and its relationship to the evolving *comedia*.

WEINBERG, BERNARD. "Robortello on the *Poetics*." In *Critics and Criticism: Ancient and Modern,* ed. R. S. Crane. Chicago: Univ. of Chicago Press, 1975.

WILSON, WILLIAM E. *Guillén de Castro.* New York: Twayne, 1973. (Twayne's World Authors Series, 253.)

WOOD, NEAL. "Some Common Aspects of the Thought of Seneca and Machiavelli." *Renaissance Quarterly,* 21 (1968), 11-23.

XIMENO, VICENTE. *Escritores del reyno de Valencia.* 2 vols. Valencia: Joseph Estevan Dolz, 1747-49.

Index

Academia de los Nocturnos, 20, 21
Aguilar, Garpas de, 19
Aguilar, Pedro de, 130n8
Allegory, 38-40, 49, 54-56
Antonio, Nicolás, 26
Araucana, La (Ercilla), 18, 36, 129n4
Aristotle, 39, 50-51, 73-74, 75, 117, 119, 124, 128, 142n53
Arróniz, Othón, 99
Arte nuevo de hacer comedias en este tiempo (Lope de Vega), 27, 28, 29-31, 113
Artieda. See Rey de Artieda
Atkinson, William C., 29-30, 82
Auerbach, Erich, 50
Austriada, La (Rufo), 18, 129n4

Bermúdez, Jerónimo, 95
Bouterwek, Frederick, 93
Bradner, Leicester, 90
Brustein, Robert, 148n48

Caballero de Olmedo, El (Lope de Vega), 110-11
Calderón de la Barca, Pedro, 75, 126, 146n31
Casa, Frank P., 143n55
Castigo sin venganza, El (Lope de Vega), 92, 135n62
Castro, Américo, 118
Castro, Guillén de, 18, 19
Cejador y Frauca, Julio, 19
Cervantes Saavedra, Miguel de, 17, 18, 19, 20, 27, 31, 60, 112, 119, 124
Charles V, 17, 60
Comedia Florisea (Avendaño), 27
Condenado por desconfiado, El (Tirso de Molina), 90
Crawford, J. P. W., 25, 27, 70, 71, 94
Curtius, Ernst, R., 120

Don Quixote de la Mancha (Cervantes), 18, 27, 119
Dostoevsky, Fyodor, 139n24
Dramas: chronology of, 25, 65-66, 89; classification of, 24-25, 30-31, 73-75, 83, 88-90, 91-96, 98-100, 110-14, 121-22, 144n21; number of acts of, 27-29, 126, 134n50

Ebersole, Alva V., 20
Edwards, Gwynne, 149-50n6
Elliott, J. H., 17
Erasmus, 20
Ethiopian History (Heliodorus), 50

Fate. See Fortune
Fernández de Moratín, Leandro, 25
Ferrer de Cardona, Luis, 19
Forcione, Alban K., 50
Fortune: and virtue, 56; contrasted with Providence, 51-53, 62-63, 64-90, 105-109; wheel of, 53, 78-81, 84, 85, 86-87, 148-49n53
Froldi, Rinaldo, 25, 65, 89, 94, 110, 122
Frye, Northrop, 103
Fucilla, Joseph G., 142n54, 147n38

Galatea, La (Cervantes), 19, 27
Genesis, 40-41, 43, 44, 45, 52, 139n25
Gerusalemme liberata (Tasso), 36, 99, 136n10
Goethe, 50
Green, Otis H., 51-52, 53
Gregory I, 49

Harris, Joseph, 54
Hauser, Arnold, 104, 153n11
Hermenegildo, Alfredo, 25, 69, 79, 80, 82, 83, 85, 88, 94, 98-99, 100, 101, 102, 103, 110, 111, 118, 124, 127-28

Index

Hero, qualities of, 49-51, 52, 55, 56, 57-58, 73-75
Hija del aire, La (Calderón), 146n31, 149-50n6
Holland, Lord, 27
Holy League, 17
Homer, 50, 73
Horace, 47, 73, 117, 119, 122, 124

Inferno (Dante), 48

John of Austria, 17, 23, 132n27
Jones, C. A., 135n62, 144n21
José Prades, Juana de, 29
Juliá Martínez, Eduardo, 20-21, 26

King Lear (Shakespeare), 49, 52-53

Laurel de Apolo, El (Lope de Vega), 19-20, 29
Lepanto, battle of, 17-18, 21, 46, 47, 57, 129n3, 131-32n23
Lewis, C. S., 119-20, 138n22, 140-41n38, 153n11
Longinus, 35
López Pinciano, Alonso, 50
Luck, 90, 109. *See also* Fortune
Lusiadas, Os (Camoens), 36

MacCurdy, Raymond R., 145n30
McKendrick, Melveena, 70, 72, 75, 83, 102, 111
Magdalene, Mary, 54, 55, 62
Mandel, Oscar, 50, 64
Maritain, Jacques, 146n32
Martí Grajales, Francisco, 19, 26
Mérimée, Henri, 25, 26, 81-82
Montserrat, Monastery of, 32, 60
Moratín. *See* Fernández de Moratín
Morel-Fatio, Alfred, 29

Odyssey, The (Homer), 35
Originality, 65, 68, 93, 95, 99, 119-20, 126-27, 134n49, 149-50n6, 153n11
Orlando furioso (Ariosto), 36, 99

Parker, Alexander A., 75, 126, 154n20
Pastor Fuster, Justo, 30
Pérez Pastor, Cristóbal, 26
Philip II, 60, 80, 105

Philip III, 60
Pierce, Frank, 26, 45-46
Pinciano, El. *See* López Pinciano
Poetry: acoustic effects of, 21-23, 34, 132n25; anaphora in, 34-35; asyndeton in, 35; hyperbaton in, 36; *in medias res* structure of, 47-48, 52, 141n38; iteration in, 35; polyptoton in, 35; rhyme in, 36-37, 125; universal-particular perspectives of, 39, 47, 117, 119, 128; versification of, 97-98, 99
Porqueras Mayo, Alberto, 115-16, 120
Providence. *See* Fortune

Reichenberger, Arnold G., 110-11, 112
Rey de Artieda, Andrés, 28
Robortello, Francesco, 74
Rojas Zorrilla, Francisco de, 114
Rosell, Cayetano, 26
Ruiz Ramón, Francisco, 25, 93-94, 110

Sargent, Cecilia V., 19, 25, 26, 68, 75, 83, 84, 93, 99-100, 101, 102, 127-28
Schiller, 50
Seneca, 30, 56, 62, 95, 98
Singleton, Charles S., 48, 137n15
Smith, Barbara Herrnstein, 115

Tasso, Torquato, 36, 38-39, 99, 136n10
Ticknor, George, 27, 33, 92-93
Tragedy. *See* Dramas, classification of
Trent, Council of, 44-45, 50
Trinkaus, Charles, 53
Trueblood, Alan S., 95

Valbuena Briones, A. J., 126, 154n20
Valbuena Prat, Angel, 95, 96
Vargas, Matías de, 23
Vega, Lope de, 18, 19, 20, 27, 28-31, 60, 91, 92, 96, 99, 110-11, 112, 113, 114, 124, 126, 127, 128
Viaje del Parnaso (Cervantes), 19, 27
Vich, Diego de, 28
Virgil, 117, 119
Virtue: in adversity, 113-14, 146n32. *See also* Fortune
Virués, Alonso de, 20
Virués, Francisco de, 20
Virués, Jerónima Agustina Benita, 20

Virués, Jerónimo de, 20
Vives, Juan Luis, 20

Wade, Gerald E., 137n11

Weinberg, Bernard, 74
Wilson, William E., 97

Ximeno, Vicente, 26